MW01221767

PEOPLE LIVE HERE

ALSO BY GEORGE F. WALKER

Prince of Naples (1971)
Ambush at Tether's End (1971)
Sacktown Rag (1972)
Zastrozzi, the Master of Discipline (1977)
Three Plays (1978)
    includes *Bagdad Saloon, Beyond Mozambique,* and *Ramona
    and the White Slaves*
Rumors of Our Death (1980)
Theatre of the Film Noir (1981)
Science and Madness (1982)
Nothing Sacred (1988)*
Suburban Motel (1997)*
    includes *Problem Child, Criminal Genius, Risk Everything, Adult
    Entertainment, Featuring Loretta,* and *The End of Civilization*
The East End Plays: Part 1 (1999)*
    includes *Criminals in Love, Better Living,* and *Escape from
    Happiness*
The East End Plays: Part 2 (1999)*
    includes *Beautiful City, Love and Anger,* and *Tough!*
The Power Plays (1999)*
    includes *Gossip, Filthy Rich,* and *The Art of War*
Somewhere Else (1999)*
Heaven (2000)*
And So It Goes (2011)*
King of Thieves (2013)*
Dead Metaphor (2015)*
    includes *Dead Metaphor, The Ravine,* and *The Burden of Self
    Awareness*
Moss Park and Tough! The Bobby and Tina Plays (2015)*
We the Family (2016)*
After Class (2017)*
    includes *Parents Night* and *The Bigger Issue*

* Published by Talonbooks

PEOPLE LIVE HERE

THE PARKDALE TRILOGY

THE CHANCE
HER INSIDE LIFE
KILL THE POOR

by George F. Walker

Foreword by Wes Berger

Talonbooks

Talonbooks
9259 Shaughnessy Street, Vancouver, British Columbia, Canada v6p 6r4
talonbooks.com

Talonbooks is located on xʷməθkʷəy̓əm, Sḵwx̱wú7mesh, and səl̓ilwətaʔɬ Lands.

First printing: 2019

Typeset in Minion
Printed and bound in Canada on 100% post-consumer recycled paper

Cover design by Typesmith
Interior design by andrea bennett

Talonbooks acknowledges the financial support of the Canada Council for the Arts, the Government of Canada through the Canada Book Fund, and the Province of British Columbia through the British Columbia Arts Council and the Book Publishing Tax Credit.

Rights to produce the theatrical works contained in *People Live Here: The Parkdale Trilogy,* in whole or in part, in any medium by any group, amateur or professional, are retained by the author. Interested persons are requested to contact Rena Zimmerman, Great North Artists Management Inc., 350 Dupont Street, Toronto, Ontario, m5r 1v9; telephone: 416-925-2051; email: info@gnaminc.com.

LIBRARY AND ARCHIVES CANADA CATALOGUING IN PUBLICATION

Title: People live here : the Parkdale trilogy : The chance, Her inside life, Kill the poor / by George F. Walker ; with a foreword by Wesley Berger.
Names: Walker, George F., author. | Berger, Wesley, writer of foreword.
Description: Plays.
Identifiers: Canadiana 20190099712 | ISBN 9781772012392 (SOFTCOVER)
Classification: LCC PS8595.A557 P46 2019 | DDC C812/.54—dc3

CONTENTS

Foreword by Wes Berger   vii

People Live Here: The Parkdale Trilogy

     The Chance   3

     Her Inside Life   67

     Kill the Poor   141

FOREWORD

by Wes Berger

When I was growing up I fantasized about being in theatre, but there wasn't much around me that made it seem like that could happen. In Chippawa, a working-class part of Niagara Falls, Ontario, young people were more inclined to go to bush parties or creekside bonfires for recreation or, if you were lucky enough to have a car, to cruise up and down Clifton Hill, the hub of the tourist area of the city. Somehow I found my way to Brock University in St. Catharines and took some theatre courses, but my connection to theatre still felt tenuous. It was only when I was introduced to George F. Walker's plays that the hook landed good and deep. His characters talked like my uncles, and their determination to be seen, heard, and understood, their resilience in the face of seemingly impossible circumstances, inspired me. Their concerns – poverty, family, survival, rules and laws that seemed indifferent or even hostile to people's well-being – were ones I had seen in my own life and in the lives of the people around me. For the first time, the theatre felt like a place where I might really belong.

When I was invited to write the preface for *People Live Here*, I asked myself what the three plays in Walker's *Parkdale Trilogy* have in common, apart from being set in the same low-income apartment complex. On some level, all three plays are populist fantasies of belonging and justice, grounded by the great empathy Walker feels for his characters and expresses through them, and tempered by their genuinely deep grief and pain.

Because Walker writes about working-class characters, his plays are sometimes miscategorized, and thus misjudged, as "social realism." The protagonists in this collection are all women who are marginalized by their life circumstances:

Marcie in *The Chance* by her poverty, depression, and age; Lacey in *Kill the Poor* by her poverty, history of addiction, and sex work; Violet in *Her Inside Life* by her mental illness and violent history. Is it likely that any of these women would end up with the almost-happy endings that these stories provide them? Probably not. But does that matter? Walker takes care to honestly depict these women's socio-political conditions, and to overtly critique the power structures behind them; but what really lies at the strongly beating heart of these plays is a stirring mix of the representative and the mythic.

Part of the power of these often darkly hilarious, touching, and sometime-harrowing plays is that the playwright envisions a different kind of ending for his characters. These grieving, angry, beleaguered women endure so much, but they also fight back with huge reserves of toughness, intelligence, courage, and grit. They are genuine, layered, complex characters, and they are also inspirational folk heroes. In these works, Walker not only moves people who would normally be on the margins to centre stage, he gives them a fighting chance at winning. I love them all so much, I want to believe they might.

PEOPLE LIVE HERE

THE
PARKDALE
TRILOGY

TOP: Fiona Reid (Marcie), Claire Burns (Jo), and Anne van Leeuwen (Amie) in *The Chance* at the Assembly Theatre in Toronto, Ontario (October 12 to 28, 2017). All photographs by John Gundy, used with permission.

BOTTOM: Anne van Leeuwen (Amie) and Claire Burns (Jo).

THE CHANCE

PRODUCTION HISTORY

The Chance was first produced by Leroy Street Theatre at the Assembly Theatre in Toronto, Ontario, Canada, from October 12 to 28, 2017, with the following cast and crew:

MARCIE	Fiona Reid
JO	Claire Burns
AMIE	Anne van Leeuwen
Director	Wes Berger
Assistant Director	Martha Moldaver
Stage Manager	Lin-Mei Lay
Producers	Chris Bretecher and Melissa Wright
Production Manager	Melissa Wright
Set Designer	Chris Bretecher
Lighting Designer	Steve Vargo
Sound Designer	Tim Lindsay
Costume Designer	Laura-Rose MacPhee
Photographer	John Gundy

SETTING

A one-bedroom apartment in a low-income high-rise.

CHARACTERS

MARCIE, fifty-six
JO, twenty-three, Marcie's daughter
AMIE, twenty-three, Jo's co-worker

THE CHANCE

A one-bedroom apartment in a low-income high-rise. MARCIE, *fifty-six, comes in from the kitchen, talking on her cellphone.*

MARCIE: (*on the phone*) It doesn't matter if it's legal for you to raise it that much. I can't pay it… Of course I'm sure. I'd have to make at least ten dollars an hour more to pay that much… Well, if you want to ask my boss for me, go ahead. I mean, I guess I could win the lottery, but since I can't afford to buy a ticket… What kind of action?… You mean I'll be evicted… Sure, you have another choice. Your other choice would be to just give me a break… Yes. You can… All you have to do is behave like a decent human being!

She disconnects. JO, *her twenty-three-year-old daughter, comes out of the bathroom and heads for the kitchen.*

MARCIE: How are you feeling?

JO: Okay…

MARCIE: Is that a lie?

JO: (*making coffee*) Yeah…

MARCIE: You should stop drinking. At least for a while. Give your body a break. It'd be the smart thing to do. (*no response*) So will you?

JO: (*from the kitchen*) Probably not.

MARCIE: Then you'll keep suffering.

JO: But I'll keep enjoying myself too. So it's a saw-off.

MARCIE: Who was that you had in here last night?

JO: His name was Greg.

MARCIE: Craig?

JO: No. Greg. Or maybe Craig, yeah.

MARCIE: Did you meet him at work?

JO: Yeah.

MARCIE: So he was a customer.

JO: He's a friend of Amie's. She introduced us.

MARCIE: So he wasn't a customer.

JO: He was both. Her friend *and* a customer.

MARCIE: I thought you weren't going to have anything more to do with men who go to that place.

JO: That's right. But –

MARCIE: He was a friend of Amie's. Got it.

JO: Are you upset that I brought him back here? We tried not to make too much noise.

MARCIE: You mean when you were screwing your brains out on my couch. Why didn't you go to his place?

JO: He's in the middle of a divorce.

MARCIE: Meaning what?

JO: His wife is still in the house.

MARCIE: And even though the marriage is over, he thinks bringing a stripper home might be a little much.

JO: He didn't want to upset her. They're negotiating the terms of their –

MARCIE: Is that why she's divorcing him? Because he goes to the clubs?

JO: Maybe.

MARCIE: You're really just letting it go, aren't you?

JO: Letting what go?

MARCIE: Any bit of common sense or decency you might have left.

JO: Well, I'm trying. You want coffee?

MARCIE: This isn't going to help. This way of looking at things.

JO: I'm trying not to look at things at all, Mum. I'm just *doing* things, okay.

MARCIE: Stupid things. Stupid and –

JO: Do you want coffee or not?

MARCIE: You think you're going to jail, don't you.

JO: Coffee, Mum. Yes or no.

MARCIE: Yes. Coffee would be nice. Thank you. And a piece of toast.

JO: Sure...

She brings the coffee and returns to the kitchen.

MARCIE: You might not, you know. You might get community service. Then you could go back to school and –

JO: What do you want on this?

MARCIE: Sorry?

JO: Your toast. You want jam?

MARCIE: Yes, please. And margarine. Anyway what good does it do to dwell on the bad things?

JO: I'm not dwelling. (*bringing toast*) I'm preparing.

MARCIE: Sounds like you're giving up

JO: I'm preparing *to* give up. If I have to serve time I want to be –

MARCIE: Numb...

JO: What?

MARCIE: Numb. You want to be numb. I get that but be careful you don't take it too far. Total numbness might be hard to recover from. (*eating*) I like this jam better when it's refrigerated.

JO: I'll keep that in mind. I gotta get ready. I'm working the lunch hour.

JO starts off.

MARCIE: Yeah, what a thing that is. Men eating their lunch while you shake your ass in their faces … Oh I found your boyfriend's wallet in the couch. (*holding it up*) Must have fallen out when –

JO: Just put it on the table, I'll take it with me when I –

MARCIE: Man's got a lot of credit cards.

JO: You looked?

MARCIE: Why not?

JO: Was there any cash?

MARCIE: Yeah. Four hundred bucks.

JO: Okay. You can keep that. He probably won't miss it.

MARCIE: He might.

JO: No. He was pretty wasted. Just keep it, buy yourself something nice.

MARCIE: I'll put it towards the rent.

JO: I gave you money for the rent.

MARCIE: I used it for hydro, and the car insurance.

JO: Buy yourself something. I'll bring more for the rent when I finish my shift.

MARCIE: Big tippers, are they? The men who eat their lunch there.

JO: Some of them. (*leaving*) Depends.

MARCIE: On what?

JO: How well I fake it, I guess.

> *JO goes into the bathroom.* MARCIE *opens the wallet and takes out the money. She starts looking at all the credit cards. Finds a folded paper. Unfolds it. Looks closely at it.*
>
> MARCIE's *phone rings. She answers it.*

MARCIE: (*on the phone*) Speaking... (*a long listening pause*) Okay... Okay, I heard what you said. But I don't know what I can do about that... If it's accumulating, its accumulating... Well, maybe you could suspend the interest until I catch up... Well, who would I have to talk to if I wanted that to happen?... You just told me *you* couldn't do that... So no one can then... Right... But if you don't, I'll never catch up, and eventually I'll get so sick of owing you that much that I'll probably just kill myself... No, it wasn't a threat. It was an idea. Look, I need a break here... I got sick and wasn't able to work for almost a year. It wasn't an actual sickness. It was grief. I lost my partner... Yeah, thanks. Anyway, that meant that I had to live on my credit cards and... Excuse me. I wasn't finished... Finished explaining how I got myself in this mess. But if that doesn't matter... Okay, if it doesn't matter *enough*... Nothing... It means I can give you nothing... Not this month.

> *A knock on the door.*

JO: (*from the bathroom*) I'll get it.

> JO *heads for the door.*

MARCIE: Because this month is when I have to pay my Visa bill. Next month is when I was planning to pay *you* something... I don't know. Maybe a hundred. Maybe a little more... No, not for sure. But I'll try.

JO comes in with AMIE, her co-worker.

MARCIE: Look, it's been great talking to you, but I have to go. The plumber's here.

She disconnects.

JO: Who was that?

MARCIE: Mastercard.

JO: They hassling you?

MARCIE: I'm a little behind.

AMIE: You want some advice about how to handle those credit card companies? Tell them to go fuck themselves. They're all thieving bastards.

MARCIE: Yes, they are. But I'm trying to hold on to some kind of half-decent credit rating.

AMIE: Why?

JO: She wants to buy a house.

AMIE: Really?

MARCIE: Just a small one. And I need to qualify for a mortgage.

AMIE: With what you make? Good luck.

MARCIE: How do you know what I make?

AMIE: Because I worked at Walmart too, remember? And you're on reduced shifts, aren't you?

MARCIE: Just for another couple of weeks.

JO: It's a suspension.

MARCIE: An unjust suspension.

AMIE: So was mine.

JO: Not really. Tell her how often you showed up for work high.

AMIE: Yeah, I could do that, or I could continue to give her my input on buying a house. (*to MARCIE*) It's a lost cause. Totally out of the question. I'm sorry, but that's definitely the truth as far as I see it. (*to JO*) I mean, unless you can convince Ruben to chip in.

MARCIE: Who's Ruben?

AMIE: The new man in her life.

MARCIE: You told me his name is Craig.

JO: Right. (*to AMIE*) It's Ruben?

AMIE: Yeah. Unless there's some other guy named Craig you've been seeing.

JO: I, ah ... No. Just him. Why would he tell me his name's Craig?

MARCIE: Or Greg.

JO: Right. Or Greg.

AMIE: I don't know. But I know him as Ruben. Ruben Joseph. And he's loaded. (*to JO*) He's in real estate. I mean, that's what he told me.

MARCIE: Maybe that's just what he tells people.

JO: Instead of what?

MARCIE: Instead of what he really does, who he really is. Do people in real estate take payments in cheques made out to cash?

JO: What are you talking about?

MARCIE: (*taking out a cheque*) I found this in his wallet. Your friend has a cheque like that from someone named Dean Olsen for $300,000.

JO: (*taking the cheque*) This was in his wallet?

MARCIE: Uh-huh.

JO: And you took it. I mean, it didn't just fall out. You didn't find it on the floor. You actually took it from his wallet.

MARCIE: Yeah.

JO: Why, Mum?

MARCIE: Might be because you were having sex with him on my couch. Maybe it made me feel like I kind of knew him or something.

AMIE: That makes sense.

MARCIE: Thanks, dear. (*to JO*) So?

JO: What?

MARCIE: Three hundred thousand dollars? Is that someone owing him a real estate commission?

JO: I don't know. Maybe.

MARCIE: And giving him that kind of cheque for it? That's normal?

JO: No. Probably not. But –

MARCIE: He's a criminal.

JO: Mum.

AMIE: Actually he might be. I mean, if it's a commission or some kind of fee, why isn't it made out to him?

MARCIE: He sounds ... risky. He's a risky individual for sure. (*to JO*) You can't be going around with someone like that just before your sentencing hearing. (*to AMIE*) Tell her.

AMIE: (*to JO*) She's probably right. I mean, I've only known him for a few weeks so –

MARCIE: I thought you went to school with him.

AMIE: No. No, that was Rick, his friend. (*off* MARCIE's *look*) What? We were all drunk. What's it matter? This guy. The other guy.

JO: Well, when you put it that way ... Jesus. (*to* MARCIE) Give me that. (*off her look*) The wallet ... and that cheque.

MARCIE: You're gonna give it back to him?

JO: Yeah. Hand it over.

MARCIE: Normally I'd have no problem doing that but –

JO: Mum?

MARCIE: Are you at least going to ask him for a reward?

JO: For finding it in our couch?

MARCIE: *My* couch. I found it in my couch. It could have belonged to anyone.

JO: Anyone?

MARCIE: Anyone you've had over in the two months you've been staying here. And most of them are long gone, right? So me knowing that, there would've been no reason to even mention it. (*to* AMIE) Right?

AMIE: She's got a point.

JO: No, she doesn't. It's too much, Mum. It won't fly. So hand them over.

> MARCIE *just looks at her.*

JO: Mum?

MARCIE: I'm a little desperate, honey. Couldn't you just ask for me?

JO: Ask what?

MARCIE: If I can get a reward.

AMIE: That might be kinda awkward.

MARCIE: Why? She could just say, "My mum found this and she'd like a little something." All he can say is no.

AMIE: No, he could say some other things too.

JO: He could say, "Is your mum fucking nuts?"

MARCIE: And you could say, "Yeah. But she'd still like a reward."

JO: We gotta go.

AMIE: No. We don't. I tried to call you but –

MARCIE: I've been on the phone, so –

AMIE: There was a fire at work.

JO: When?

AMIE: Last night. Or maybe early this morning. Anyway the club's closed.

JO: Really? For how long?

AMIE: Forever. The place burned down.

JO: Jesus…

AMIE: Yeah, it sucks.

JO: Right. It does.

MARCIE: Or maybe it doesn't. Maybe it's good. You could take it as an opportunity to try something else.

AMIE: I don't know if any of the other clubs are hiring. Out near the airport maybe.

MARCIE: I didn't say some*where* else. I said some*thing* else. You don't have to twirl around that stupid pole naked forever.

AMIE: Who said we did? I'm going to cooking school.

JO: And I'm going to jail.

AMIE: (*to MARCIE*) Yeah. So there you go.

15

MARCIE: She's not necessarily going to jail.

AMIE: Well, where else do they put convicted kidnappers?

MARCIE: When it's their own child they've taken, they have to make concessions.

JO: Yeah. So maybe two years instead of five.

AMIE: Really? Just two? You can do that, no sweat.

JO: Ya think?

AMIE: Sure. I've done almost two when you add all my drug convictions together.

MARCIE: Not really the same thing. My eighteen months were hard on me. I still don't think I've fully recovered.

JO: Really?

MARCIE: You think it's girl party or something? Like that stupid show?

AMIE: Sometimes it is. But with a lot less sex.

MARCIE: Yeah … Anyway she could get a lot more time if they find out.

AMIE: Find out what?

MARCIE: That she's been stripping.

AMIE: That's an issue? How was she supposed to support herself?

MARCIE: By doing something else.

AMIE: Yeah but that would mean changing professions.

MARCIE: It's not a profession.

AMIE: Then what is it?

JO: If I'm gonna have to do more time, I think I'll just grab Suzy again and take off.

MARCIE: There's that bad part of your brain talking to you again.

JO: I'm just saying…

AMIE: Yeah, she's just talkin' about something she'd like to do but probably wouldn't.

JO: Unless I would.

MARCIE: Well, I wouldn't let you.

JO: You couldn't stop me. Look, you've got enough going on, so don't worry about what I do, okay.

MARCIE: You think I can stop worrying about what you do? Just like that? Don't be stupid. Even with all the other things I've got on my mind, I still –

AMIE: Money problems again?

MARCIE: Yeah. What else? That's all I've ever had. Money problems.

AMIE: (*sitting*) I can lend you a few hundred.

MARCIE: Every day?

AMIE: What?

MARCIE: Three hundred dollars every day for three years. That's what it's gonna take to get me in a good-enough situation.

AMIE: Good enough for what?

JO: To buy a house.

MARCIE: Like you were already told.

AMIE: I thought you dropped that idea.

MARCIE: When?

AMIE: When I told you it couldn't happen.

MARCIE: So you're like my financial advisor now?

JO: She's right, Mum. Anyone would tell you the same.

MARCIE: Well, if it's all right with you, I'll wait until I'm in a position to have the bank tell me. In the meantime both of you should stop stepping on my dreams.

AMIE's cellphone rings. She answers it.

AMIE: (*on the phone*) Hey, Rick. What's up?... Yeah I heard. It sucks big time... What?... Wow, that's...

JO: What is it?

AMIE: Three people died in that fire...

JO: Who were they?

AMIE: (*on the phone*) You know who they were?... Jesus.

JO: Who?

AMIE: The Riley brothers.

MARCIE: The owners?

JO: Yeah... (*to AMIE*) Who else?

AMIE: (*on the phone*) Who's the third?... Oh. Okay. You all right?... Okay. Well... Yeah. Later.

She disconnects.

AMIE: The other one was Ruben.

JO: What?

JO seems a little shaken.

AMIE: He hung around to play pool with the Riley brothers. And they got trapped in the basement.

MARCIE: I don't get it. How could he be there when he was here?

JO: Not all night. He left around two I think.

JO sits. Stands. Sits again.

AMIE: You okay?

JO: Not really. (*looking at the couch*) It's kinda –

MARCIE's cellphone goes off. She answers it.

MARCIE: (*on the phone*) Speaking... Okay. But wasn't I talking to you yesterday? You think my situation's changed since then? ... How much more? ... Okay, but it doesn't really matter that there's additional interest because I can't pay it, right? ... Okay, well, I appreciate you letting me know, I guess... Thank you. And you have a good day as well.

She disconnects.

MARCIE: Can I see that wallet?

JO: Why?

MARCIE: Just hand it over, okay.

JO obeys. MARCIE digs out the cheque.

MARCIE: Is there any way this could still be of value?

JO: He's dead, Mum.

MARCIE: I meant to us. I think cheques made out to cash are just like money. I mean, anyone can use them, right?

JO: Mum.

MARCIE puts the cheque on the coffee table in front of the couch.

MARCIE: Let's just think about that for a while.

They are all looking at the cheque. MARCIE's cellphone goes off.

MARCIE: (*answering*) Can't talk now. Call back next week.

She disconnects.

JO: I'm scared, Mum. (*off the cheque*) You're going to try to cash it, aren't you?

MARCIE: Well, someone should cash it.

AMIE: It belongs to Ruben Joseph.

MARCIE: He's dead.

AMIE: He mighta told the guy who gave it to him.

MARCIE: Told him what?

AMIE: That he lost it. You know, so the guy who gave it to him could put a stop payment on it.

JO: Or he might have told the Rileys. Maybe that's why he went there so early this morning. To look for it.

MARCIE: Not to play pool, you mean.

JO: No...

MARCIE: Have you checked your cell this morning? He might have texted you.

> JO's leather jacket is on a chair. She pulls her cellphone out of a pocket.

AMIE: Can you put a hold on a cheque made out to cash?

MARCIE: I don't think so...

JO: (*off her cellphone*) Yeah there's a text. He wanted to know if he left his wallet here.

MARCIE: You should answer it.

JO: He's dead.

MARCIE: Answer it anyway. We should have it on record that he didn't leave it here. (*to AMIE*) Google it.

AMIE: What?

MARCIE: "Can you put a stop payment on a cheque made out to cash?"

JO: I don't like what's happening, Mum. You're trying to put something in motion here.

MARCIE: It's a simple investigation of the facts and possibilities.

AMIE is googling.

JO: Which makes me feel like you're about to do something stupid.

MARCIE: Just relax. We're not anywhere near that yet. I'm just –

JO: Investigating. Right. Look, what we really should be doing with it is giving it to his wife.

MARCIE: Why? You think she needs it?

JO: I don't know. And that's beside the friggin' point, Mum.

MARCIE: Says who? (*to AMIE*) So?

AMIE: Can't find anything about that. Maybe we should just try to cash it and see what happens.

JO: Jesus!

AMIE: Or we could give it to his wife.

JO: Do you know her?

AMIE: Why would I know her?

MARCIE: (*to JO*) Yeah. She just took off her clothes for him.

AMIE: Right.

MARCIE: And maybe a couple of other things?

AMIE: No. He was really into Jo.

MARCIE: Okay… (*to JO*) So you got to know each other when you were sticking your ass in his face. I guess the subject of his wife never came up then.

JO: Is this about Dad?

MARCIE: I'm sorry?

JO: Because of how he was. (*to JO*) He cheated a lot.

MARCIE: Yeah he did. But as far as I know he never did it with strippers.

JO: As far as you know.

AMIE: What's wrong with strippers? I mean, as something on the side. We're no different than other women who do that.

MARCIE: Except for the way you get introduced, like I just said. Anyway since we don't have a way to get the cheque to his wife we should just move on from that.

AMIE: I could give it to Rick. He probably knows her.

MARCIE: He also probably knows that a cheque made out to cash is the same as money. What do you think the chances are of him just cashing it himself?

AMIE: I'd have to say pretty good.

MARCIE's cellphone goes off.

MARCIE: (*answering*) Not today. Call me next week.

She disconnects.

AMIE: You owe a lot of people money, eh?

MARCIE: Not people. Companies. And they can wait. Maybe for just a little while now.

JO: Nothing you say can convince me we should do this.

MARCIE: I haven't even started trying, so don't be so sure.

JO: Jesus...

MARCIE: I haven't brought up your daughter yet, have I?

AMIE: Yeah...

JO: Whaddya mean, "yeah"?

AMIE: Well, that money could mean a fresh start for when you get out of prison.

MARCIE: Or it could mean you never have to go to prison.

JO: What?

MARCIE: You could just take off.

JO: Right. Here we go.

MARCIE: I don't like the way you said that. Have I ever advised you to break the law before?

JO: Only by having me watch you do it.

MARCIE: What they called fraud was just me being a little late paying people back. Like now.

JO: What's that mean, "like now"? You passing bad cheques again?

MARCIE: Not really.

JO: Not really, meaning?

MARCIE: I don't consider it a bad cheque if you have an honest intention to pay later on.

AMIE: Sounds like the two of you might be doing some time together.

JO: You hear that, Mum?

MARCIE: She was just kidding.

AMIE: Not really.

JO: (*to MARCIE*) If you wind up in prison, Suzy won't have either of us. It'll just be Jimmy and his idiot sister in her life.

MARCIE: All the more reason to get this cheque cashed as fast as possible. Things are kinda closing in on me.

JO: Things? You mean collection agencies?

MARCIE: I wish. No, it's Rocco.

JO: Who the fuck's Rocco?

MARCIE: He was the guy on that flyer I got a few months back. "Need money? Call Rocco"... So I did. Anyway it turns out that Rocco has a very strict payback schedule with very high interest rates.

AMIE: You mean he's a loan shark.

MARCIE: I guess you could call him that.

AMIE: There's been a guy called Rocco hanging around the club. (*to JO*) Big guy. Crazy eyes. He's a friend of Ruben's, I think.

JO: Yeah, I've seen him. (*to MARCIE*) And you owe him how much?

MARCIE: Well, the interest compounds daily, so that depends.

JO: But it's a lot.

MARCIE: A lot more than I borrowed, yeah.

JO: Jesus...

    She grabs the cheque.

MARCIE: What are you doing?

JO: You're afraid and you're desperate. And that's when you make your biggest mistakes.

MARCIE: That's when everyone makes their biggest mistakes, honey.

JO: Yours are worse. I'm gonna rip this friggin' thing up.

MARCIE: No. No, no, no. You can't do that. It's money!

JO: No, it's trouble.

AMIE: It *could* be trouble. But it's *definitely* money. And I think we should – (*to MARCIE*) Am I in for a share?

MARCIE: Sure. It's a three-way split.

AMIE: Great. And that's... eighty thousand. Okay. Yeah. (*to JO*) I'm with your mum, sweetie. Let's go for it.

MARCIE: Yeah, put it down, Jo. Let's at least talk about it some more.

JO: I don't think so.

MARCIE: Please.

AMIE: Yeah. Please.

MARCIE: Come on. Put it down. We'll just talk. Okay?

AMIE: Maybe. Maybe ... but there are conditions. You can't say I could just take off if I had money. You gotta come up with something better. You know, I couldn't leave Suzy.

MARCIE: I meant take off *with* Suzy. You got such a bad deal about her. You lost custody because you didn't have good representation.

AMIE: And a drug problem.

MARCIE: Which she was fighting.

AMIE: And losing. (*to JO*) Not all the time. But –

MARCIE: Even so, they could have given you more time. They didn't have to be so up their asses about it. They put you in a situation you might never get to fix. But if you use some of this money to get the hell away from here, you and your little girl would have a chance to make it better.

JO: For how long?

AMIE: As long as you don't get caught.

JO: Jesus ...

AMIE: I'm not saying I'm for the idea. I'm just not totally against it.

MARCIE: (*to JO*) Jo? Joanna?

JO: I'm thinking ...

> *MARCIE sneaks a look to AMIE.*

MARCIE: Okay, but be brave in your thinking.

AMIE is edging closer to JO from behind.

JO: Whatever that means.

MARCIE: Well, is this all we want out of our lives? Places like this to live in? Jobs in places like Walmart or shitty strip clubs? Please, honey... things like this don't drop into your hands for no reason.

JO: What are you talking about?

MARCIE: Well, maybe it's God's will.

JO: God's will. Oh gimme a break, okay?

AMIE suddenly throws her arms around JO from behind, pinning both of JO's arms to her side.

JO: Hey!

MARCIE gently takes the cheque from JO's hand.

MARCIE: There we go...

AMIE lets JO loose.

JO: (*to AMIE*) What the fuck?

AMIE: I couldn't help it. It just came to me.

JO: What? What came to you?

AMIE: A little pastry shop. You know, cakes, cupcakes, maybe some sweet rolls. I could start something like that for myself.

MARCIE: Yes, you could. That's smart thinking, Amie. (*to JO*) You should try thinking like that.

JO: Like what? Like starting a pastry shop?

AMIE: Sure. As long as it wasn't across the street from mine.

MARCIE: I was talking about getting yourself into a better situation.

JO: By taking my kid and disappearing.

MARCIE: Well, I'd know where you were.

AMIE: Me too. Look, this sentencing hearing is gonna be rough. Jimmy's a lying douche and he's going to say all kinds of shit about you.

MARCIE: Right. So let's consider all that. Rocco and the possibility he's gonna start squeezing me big time for his money, Amie's pastry shop dream, and the serious amount of prison time you could get ... and give those things the weight they deserve. Okay? In the meantime I'll just put it back where it was, okay?

MARCIE puts the cheque back. And they all look at it (and each other) again.

JO's cell goes off. She answers it.

JO: (*on the phone*) Hi ... Yeah, I heard ... No. It's never opening again ... Well, what's that's to you, Jimmy?

MARCIE: What's his problem?

JO: He's worried I won't make my support payments.

AMIE: Asshole.

MARCIE: Yeah. Tell him *you're* worried he's too stupid to be a human being. That he's just some kind of dumb animal who has no right being anywhere near his daughter let alone in charge of her well-being. No, let me do it. (*grabbing the phone*) Listen up, idiot. Don't worry about your damn support payments. You've got no right to be even asking that question ... Right. But the judge was an idiot who didn't take into consideration all the times you were out of work and didn't contribute a cent ... Hey! Hey!! I wasn't finished, you pathetic turd. Just do your job, take care of my granddaughter, and don't worry about sucking any more money out of Jo or you'll be getting a visit from a friend of mine ... No. Not one of my "lesbo pals." This guy will be a whole other kind of scary to you ... Yes, you are. Yes, you are afraid of lesbians, you limp-dicked clown. So back off! Or you'll be having to deal with my pal Rocco and that's something you might not survive!!

She hands the phone back to JO.

AMIE: Rocco? You're gonna set Rocco on him?

MARCIE: If I have to.

AMIE: And how will Rocco be getting paid to do that?

MARCIE: Well, money might not be a concern, right?

JO: (*on the phone*) Yeah, well, she hates your guts, so whaddya expect? Look, put Suzy on, okay? ... Just do it. I need to talk to her.

MARCIE: How she got involved with that fool I'll never understand.

AMIE: Me either. And I've had my share of fools. Maybe we both should have switched teams like you did. Sheila never treated you bad, did she?

MARCIE: No. She just died on me.

JO: (*on the phone*) Hi Sweetie. How's my girl ...?

JO heads into the kitchen.

MARCIE: Look, I need you to share the load on this thing, okay?

AMIE: Well, who got her in that bear hug?

MARCIE: Yeah, that was good. But I was talking about persuasion. You need to make it clear that the rewards outweigh the risks.

AMIE: Even if I'm not sure they do? The risks could be really big and they could come from a lot of different places. The cops. And suppose that Dean Olsen guy's connected and he finds out that we –

MARCIE: How long do you think men are going to be paying to have you do what you do for them? Look, that pastry shop thing is nice and all that. It's a nice idea. But how about just having a choice?

AMIE: A choice about what?

MARCIE: To do that. Or to do something else. Just another job. Like maybe you could get that headstone for your mother's grave you say you want so bad. Or maybe even an apartment of your own instead of that dumpy house you share with all those other "entertainers."

AMIE: It's okay there. I like most of the girls. But yeah, a little privacy would be nice…

MARCIE: I'm not saying your future isn't in pastries but –

AMIE: Yeah, there's other things too.

MARCIE: Quality-of-life things. A headstone for your mum would make you feel a lot better about yourself.

AMIE: Whaddya mean?

MARCIE: Well, you were basically a shit daughter to her.

AMIE: I guess.

MARCIE: No need to guess. You broke her heart.

AMIE: She told you that?

MARCIE: Yeah. She told me that a lot. Well, did you expect her to be over the moon about what you did for a living?

AMIE: No, but –

MARCIE: Did she ever accept money from you?

AMIE: No…

MARCIE: And I know you offered. She didn't like it, Amie. She didn't like it at all.

AMIE: Yeah, okay. But she never tried to make me ashamed of it either. Like you're trying to do.

MARCIE: You think that's what I'm –

AMIE: There are worse things I could be doing. I'm not hurting anyone. And that's something, isn't.it? I've met guys at the club who brag about how they swing deals that screw a lot of people out of their money. I'm a better person than they are, right?

MARCIE: Some serial killers are better persons than they are. The point is –

AMIE's cell goes off. She answers it.

AMIE: (*on the phone*) Hey, Rick… Yeah, I'm there now… I don't know, I'll ask. (*covering the speaker*) He wants to know if Ruben left his wallet here.

MARCIE gestures something which says, "Are you an idiot?"

AMIE: (*on the phone*) No. They haven't seen it… Who's asking?… Yeah, but besides you?… How does she know he lost it?

MARCIE gestures.

AMIE: (*covering the speaker*) The cops told his wife it wasn't on his body. (*on the phone*) Well, it's not here, so –… Yeah, I'm sure… Yeah, honest. Jeez… Hey Rick, was Ruben really in real estate?… Just curious… Yeah. Okay, it's none of.my business. Got it… I said I got it! (*disconnecting*) Snotty little prick.

MARCIE: He didn't like that question, eh. So maybe Ruben wasn't in real estate.

AMIE: I never thought he was.

MARCIE: You said just the opposite a while ago.

AMIE: Sometimes I say the opposite just so I can hear how it sounds.

MARCIE: You mean if it sounds like the truth.

AMIE: Yeah.

MARCIE: And it didn't.

AMIE: What didn't? What I said then? Or what I said just now.

MARCIE: Then.

AMIE: Yeah, that was wrong. No way he's in real estate. But so what?

MARCIE: So we gotta do this right now.

> *MARCIE grabs the cheque and heads for the door.*

AMIE: Where you goin'?

MARCIE: There's a bank down the block.

AMIE: I think this could be a big mistake.

MARCIE: Well, if I don't come back, you'll know you were right.

> *MARCIE hurries out. JO comes out of the kitchen, putting her cell away.*

JO: She's got a cold but it doesn't sound too – Where's my mother?

AMIE: Off to the bank.

JO: (*noticing*) With the cheque.

AMIE: I guess she got tired of trying to convince you. What's up with that, anyway? You've always been up for taking a chance on things. Ever since we were kids, even.

JO: And look where it's got me. Nowhere. (*punching a number on her cell*) She probably won't answer.

AMIE: That'll be my bet.

JO hangs up. MARCIE's phone goes off in the room.

JO: That's hers.

> *JO finds it under a cushion where MARCIE was sitting. JO looks at AMIE, who shrugs. JO answers the phone.*

JO: (*on the phone*) Hi... No, it's her daughter... Okay... Okay, I understand... Yeah, I'll tell her...

> *She disconnects.*

AMIE: Who was that?

JO: Rocco.

AMIE: Rocco, the loan shark? What'd he want?

JO: He wanted me to tell my mum that after this time it gets much worse.

AMIE: What does?

> *MARCIE opens the door and comes in. Her nose is bleeding.*

JO: (*pointing*) That?

AMIE: (*looking*) Ah, shit.

MARCIE: I'm going to need a little tending to here.

AMIE: (*heading to the bathroom*) I'll get a wet cloth.

MARCIE: Good idea. (*reaching out to JO*) Give me a hand, honey. I'm a little dizzy.

> *JO helps her to the couch.*

MARCIE: Must be in shock. (*sitting*) That guy was very efficient. (*off her face*) All this took maybe three seconds.

JO: It was a message. From Rocco. There's more to come if he doesn't get his money. How much do you owe him?

MARCIE: Is it after 2 p.m.?

JO: Yeah.

MARCIE: Then it's just under ten thousand.

JO: You borrowed ten grand from the guy?!

MARCIE: Six. But like I said, the interest is –

JO: Holy fuck, Mum.

MARCIE: Yeah. It's a mess. I owe everyone. Plus I still haven't paid for Sheila's funeral. And that's bothering me more than anything. She'd hate owing that.

JO: Well, she's dead, so she doesn't know about it, does she?

MARCIE: You're sure of that, are you?

JO: Yes.

MARCIE: Sheila was right. A little religion could have helped you calm down and make better choices.

JO: Has it helped you?

MARCIE: It came to me too late.

JO: Yeah. Look, I liked Sheila, Mum. I appreciated that she helped you pull it together after Dad fucked off. But all that God stuff she was into meant nothing to me.

MARCIE: Why not though?

JO: Let's just say I didn't know how he fit in. So… she didn't have insurance? I mean, not even enough to take care of the funeral?

MARCIE: She cashed it in.

JO: Why?

MARCIE: To pay for the lawyer.

JO: Why'd she need a lawyer?

MARCIE: *Your* lawyer.

JO: She paid for my lawyer? I thought I was on legal aid.

MARCIE: You were wrong. I mean, it ran out.

JO: I never asked her to do that.

MARCIE: Not directly.

JO: Meaning what?

MARCIE: Well, she knew you spent all your money on booze and weed, so if you weren't doing that she wouldn't have had to –

JO: I was depressed.

MARCIE: I know.

JO: I'd lost custody of my daughter.

MARCIE: Right. So someone had to step up. And that was Sheila.

JO: Ah, man…

> AMIE *returns with a cloth and begins to wipe* MARCIE*'s face.*

AMIE: This Rocco guy doesn't fool around, eh?

MARCIE: Yeah. Under different circumstances he'd be a valuable friend.

JO: What's that mean?

MARCIE: Well, we might need some protection. Suppose the guy who gave Ruben that cheque is not a respectable person. Suppose he thinks he's not gonna be out that money now. Then he finds out we cashed it.

JO: Which we haven't done yet, have we?

MARCIE: I didn't even get close to the bank. The guy blindsided me on the sidewalk and just kept moving.

JO: Well then…

MARCIE: Yeah. We need to think this through in a whole other way.

AMIE: So you don't want to cash it?

MARCIE: When did I say that? I meant we need to come up with a more detailed plan for when we do. This should have been on my mind all along.

JO: What?

MARCIE: That we all have to take off out of here. (*to AMIE*) Does it really matter where you start baking cupcakes?

AMIE: I guess not. But I've never lived anywhere else.

MARCIE: Yeah. And look how far that's gotten you. (*to JO*) And you and Suzy needed to get away from here a long time ago. Away from your ex. Away from your dealers. And away from all the dead-enders you meet in bars. Yeah. We'll go somewhere. We'll all start off as new people. No obligations. Just possibilities. Man, I'm excited!

Her cell rings. She finds it where JO put it down and answers it.

MARCIE: (*on the phone*) Fuck off.

JO: Who was that?

MARCIE: Who cares.

She takes the cheque out of her pocket.

MARCIE: (*heading for the door*) Let me try this again.

JO: Whoa!

JO moves to intercept her. AMIE stops her.

AMIE: Let her go. She's got a point. I mean, I've been thinking.

JO: It's too late.

AMIE: For what?

JO: For you to start thinking.

AMIE: That's a crappy thing to say, Jo.

JO: It's true. All you've done your whole life is follow me. I quit school. You quit school. I started stripping. Two months later you were in that club doing it, too. You just do what I do, so where's the thinking in that.

AMIE: Yeah, well I thought it would be better to get an abortion when I got knocked up. I thought it would be better to stop getting thrown in jail by getting off junk. I thought I needed help to do that. And I did.

JO: Yeah, okay. I'm sorry. But –

AMIE: We should do what she says we should. I *think* it's the best thing for all of us.

MARCIE: So can I go to the bank now?

MARCIE's phone goes off again.

MARCIE: (*on the phone*) I told you to – ... What? ... I don't know what you're talking about. What's your name? ... That name doesn't sound familiar to me.

JO: Who is it?

MARCIE: (*covering the speaker*) It's Dean Olsen.

JO: Shit.

AMIE: Who's that?

JO: The guy who signed the cheque.

AMIE: (*to MARCIE*) Hang up.

JO: No. (*to MARCIE*) Find out what he wants.

AMIE: Yeah. And then hang up.

MARCIE: (*to JO and AMIE*) He wants to talk about it.

AMIE: The cheque? How do you know?

MARCIE: He just told me.

AMIE: Hang up.

MARCIE: (*on the phone*) Like I said, I don't know what you're talking about ... Okay. Go ahead ...

JO: Go ahead with what?

MARCIE: (*to JO*) He's telling me all the things that could happen to us if we don't give it back ...

JO: You mean he just assumes we have it?

MARCIE: Yeah.

AMIE: Hang up. Please hang up. Please!

MARCIE: (*to AMIE*) Shh. I'm trying to listen ... (*on the phone*) Can you repeat that last thing? ... Really? You think you'll get away with that?

JO: Away with what?

MARCIE: (*to JO*) You don't need to know. (*on the phone*) Finished? ... Good. Now let me tell you a little something about who you're dealing with here.

AMIE: No. Don't. Don't tell him anything. Just hang up!

MARCIE: (*to AMIE*) Shh!

AMIE: (*to JO*) That name. Dean Olsen. It sounds familiar. And not in a good way.

JO: Mum?

MARCIE: (*on the phone*) I was born in 1958. I was orphaned in 1959 when both my parents were killed in a car crash. And nothing about my life since then has been easy. I was started ... No, I won't shut the fuck up. You need to know – What, now? ... Okay ...

> She walks to the window. Looks out.

MARCIE: I see two men. Which one are you? Okay, so who's the other one? ... Rick who?

AMIE: What?

AMIE and JO rush to the window.

MARCIE: (*to AMIE and JO*) You know them?

JO: Yeah.

AMIE: The one on the left is Rick.

JO: And the other one is ...

AMIE and JO: Ruben.

MARCIE: Ruben, the dead guy.

AMIE and JO: Yeah ...

MARCIE: (*on the phone*) Okay, what's going on? ... I don't think that's a good idea. (*to AMIE and JO*) They want to come up and talk.

AMIE: Hang up.

JO: Is that really your only suggestion?

AMIE: You got a better one? I don't think we should have even admitted that they're actually there. Especially not Ruben. That was a big mistake. Opening up communications was a really fucking big mistake. Guys like Rick, that's all they need. An opening.

JO: An opening to do what?

AMIE: You know what.

JO: No. What?

AMIE: Fuck with our heads. That's what? (*whispering*) Hang up ...

MARCIE: Don't you even want to know why the guy who's supposed to be dead ... isn't?

AMIE: No ... They're experts at fucking with people's heads. Even from a distance, like now. Imagine what they can do close up.

JO: Just tell them we need time to consider it.

MARCIE: If they can come up?

JO: Yeah ...

MARCIE: That'll make it sound like we have something to hide.

JO: We do.

AMIE: She's right.

MARCIE: Well, I have to tell them something.

AMIE: No! You don't. Just hang the fuck up!!

> *MARCIE shrugs and disconnects. They are all looking down onto the street.*

JO: They don't look happy.

> *JO's cell goes off.*

MARCIE: He's calling again.

JO: That's mine.

AMIE: Don't ...

JO: Be quiet ... (*answering the phone*) Hi, Ruben. You look pretty good for a dead guy ... at least from this far away. What's that all about anyway? ... You're dead, you're not dead. I mean, come on. Make up your mind.

AMIE: (*still looking out*) Doesn't look like he's laughing.

JO: (*covering the speaker*) No. He must think it's pretty serious stuff. (*on the phone*) Does your wife know? ... That you're alive, what else ... (*covering the speaker*) It's "none of my fucking business."

AMIE: Maybe he's right. Maybe you should just wish him well and end the conversation. I'm hungry. (*heading into the kitchen*) Anyone else want a sandwich or something?

MARCIE: (*to JO*) Ask him if he needs the money because he's starting a new life. (*off JO's look*) Just a thought.

JO: (*on the phone*) Does anyone else know you're actually alive, Ruben? ... Okay. (*to MARCIE*) He's not here to talk about that. He's here to get that cheque back "one way or another."

MARCIE: Ask him whose body it was they found.

JO: I don't want to know that.

MARCIE: Why not?

JO: Well, suppose it was a friend of mine.

MARCIE: You had friends in that club?

JO: Yeah. The bouncers. Some of my customers.

MARCIE: Okay, and you don't want to know if they killed one of those people to cover up ... what they're doing?

JO: Which is allowing him to start a whole new life?

MARCIE: Well, it makes sense if you think about it. The cheque is made out to cash, so he wouldn't need to show ... identification.

JO: What are you talking about?

MARCIE: Hey, get with the plot here. It's the only explanation.

JO: Ham and cheese okay?

MARCIE: And tell him there's no way we're returning that cheque. And that we – (*grabbing JO's phone*) We have a lot less to lose by calling the cops, you know. So knock it off with the threats ... Now calm down and get it together. I've got a suggestion.

AMIE: Mustard?

MARCIE: A deal... We make a deal... (*to* JO) No deals. Just the cheque.

JO: Ask him if that was actually Rick on the phone before pretending to be Dean Olsen.

MARCIE: He heard that. And that's also "none of our fucking business."

AMIE: (*from the kitchen*) Dean Olsen. Yeah. I just remembered who he is. He's that –

JO: Right. He's that guy who was putting pressure on the Rileys to sell him the club. (*on the phone*) Is Dean Olsen dead, Ruben?

AMIE: What? Don't go there?

JO: Is his body the one you put in there after you set that fire?

AMIE: Whoa. Whoa! Don't ask him that? Take that back. Tell him we don't give a shit about that.

MARCIE: I do. We need to keep pushing... get them back on their heels.

AMIE: No, that'll just make them more dangerous. I think we should just hand over the cheque. We're in over our heads here.

MARCIE: No, we *were* in over our heads. Now I think we might be able to make it to the surface. (*to* JO) It's time to end the call. We need a strategy. (*to* AMIE) Yeah, I'd like that.

AMIE: What?

MARCIE: Mustard. (*off her look*) Okay? Can you do that now? Make those sandwiches?

AMIE: Sure.

> AMIE *heads into the kitchen.*

MARCIE: I think better on a full stomach. You know that. Now hang up.

JO: (*on the phone*) Gotta go.

> *She disconnects.* MARCIE *heads over to the couch.*

MARCIE: Okay, so how to proceed...

> JO's *phone goes off.*

MARCIE: Don't answer it.

JO: Okay.

> *A phone goes off in the kitchen.* AMIE *comes in with her phone in her hand.*

AMIE: They're calling *me* now. Why are they calling *me*? How do they even know I'm here?

JO: You told Rick.

AMIE: Yeah, but... Okay, but... that doesn't mean I'm involved. I could just be visiting. They think I'm in this with you.

JO: You are.

AMIE: Am I? Really? I mean, I was up for it in some way but –

MARCIE: You wanted the money.

AMIE: Yes. I did. But now...

> *Her phone stops ringing.*

MARCIE: Stay strong, Amie. Keep thinking about a better future. We just need to –

AMIE: Stay alive. We need to stay alive. That's the number one thing on my list.

MARCIE: Yeah, but not just that. We need better than just staying alive. Trust me.

> JO's *phone goes off.*

AMIE: Answer it.

JO: Now you want *me* to talk to them?

AMIE: Just to ask if I can leave.

MARCIE: Bad move. They'll just grab you.

AMIE: I can go out the back.

> *JO is looking out the window again.*

JO: It's just Ruben now?

AMIE: Where'd Rick go?

MARCIE: Guess.

AMIE: Maybe he just went away.

JO: Or maybe he went to cover the back.

> *JO's phone stops ringing.*

AMIE: Yeah. Maybe. But that's okay. I mean, he likes me, so he'll probably just let me leave. (*off their looks*) Okay, let's call the cops.

MARCIE: We're not there yet.

> *MARCIE's phone goes off.*

MARCIE: My turn. (*to JO*) How did they get my number anyway?

JO: Not sure. You were my contact at work. You know, for emergencies.

MARCIE: Like what? If you fell off the stage?

JO: Yeah or –

AMIE: A girl was attacked last year.

MARCIE: In the club?

JO: No…

AMIE: When she was leaving. It was some guy she got turfed out when he started to get a little too personal.

MARCIE: Was it bad?

JO: Not really.

AMIE: He almost killed her, Jo.

JO: (*off MARCIE*) Did she need to know that?

AMIE: Sorry.

MARCIE: Almost killed her. Right. But we should just keep on with our lives, though. I should stay in crippling debt. You should keep working in jobs that put you in danger from your "customers." We should just give up, turn that $300,000 over to those guys out there, and let them be on their way. Hmm. On their way...

JO: What?

> *MARCIE answers her phone.*

MARCIE: (*on the phone*) Okay, first off, one more threat from you, we call the police, and there goes your escape money... Well, what else could it be? Did you fake your death just for fun?... (*to JO*) That got him. (*on the phone*) I'm suggesting a deal... A four-way split.

AMIE: What?

MARCIE: (*to AMIE*) I thought you wanted out.

AMIE: Only if it was going to get violent.

MARCIE: (*on the phone*) Make that a five-way split.

AMIE: Thanks...

MARCIE: (*to AMIE*) Yeah. How about those sandwiches?

> *AMIE nods and goes into the kitchen.*

MARCIE: (*on the phone*) ... Well, you'll just have to make do. Find somewhere closer to hide out ... We'll have to pull back on our plans too ... You're okay with that? Really? (*to JO*) That's a surprise. (*on the phone*) Who are you running from, anyway? ... What's that mean?

JO: Who is it?

MARCIE: (*to JO*) Himself.

JO: What the fuck does that mean?

MARCIE: Good question. (*on the phone*) You're gonna have to get back to me.

> *She disconnects.*

JO: What is it?

MARCIE: No. *Who* is it? Who is that guy down there?

JO: Really?

MARCIE: No. Practically.

> *AMIE comes in with a tray of sandwiches and pickles.*

AMIE: (*putting the tray down*) Here you go.

JO: Thanks ...

MARCIE: (*to AMIE*) Nice presentation.

JO: Mum?

MARCIE: Yeah. Just let me get some of this into my stomach.

> *MARCIE takes a bite. Chews. Swallows.*

MARCIE: Everyone thinks Ruben is dead, right? But actually it's Dean Olsen who's dead. So if Ruben plans to live as Dean, he needs ... he needs ...

AMIE: What? He needs what?

MARCIE: He needs his ... signature. He doesn't want to cash the cheque. Well, he probably would, but mostly he needs the cheque to get Dean's signature ...

JO: So he can get used to forging it.

MARCIE: And then get access to everything else Dean has.

JO: Which is probably a lot. Or it wouldn't be worth it.

MARCIE: Makes sense.

JO: So ... what does that mean to us if it's true?

MARCIE: Sheila loved dill pickles. She had cravings for them all the time. (*to JO*) Remember?

JO: Yeah ...

MARCIE: I miss her so much.

JO: Yeah. I know.

AMIE: I didn't know her that well, but she was always kind to me.

MARCIE: She felt sorry for you.

AMIE: Why?

MARCIE: For the same reason I do. You were weaned too early.

AMIE: (*to JO*) What's she talking about?

JO: You weren't breastfed long enough?

MARCIE: Not just that. She wasn't given enough ... guidance. Not that it always matters. (*to AMIE*) Jo was given lots of guidance and look at her. (*to JO*) All that trouble you had with drugs. And you were warned about that a lot. Even your father had enough on the ball to talk to you about it.

JO: (*to AMIE*) When I was ten. Just before he fucked off for good. That was his parting advice to me: "Try to stay clean for as long as possible, okay?"

MARCIE: (*to* AMIE) Maybe it's just that you seem so ... sad. More than sad. Unconnected ... Anyway, she felt sorry for you and she would have like to hear that you had something in mind for yourself. (*off her look*) You know, your little bakeshop. (*to* JO) So maybe if we just give him a peek at the cheque so he can take a picture of the signature ... But ...

JO: But what?

MARCIE: That still doesn't explain why Ruben had to appear to die or why Dean Olsen gave him that cheque ...

> MARCIE *starts to search for something in the kitchen drawers.*

JO: What is it, Mum?

MARCIE: He has associates.

JO: Who does?

MARCIE: There was a list of them on the flyer. Made the whole thing look more legitimate.

> MARCIE *finds the flyer.*

MARCIE: Which one of you thought Rocco was a friend of Ruben's?

AMIE: Me. But I was just –

> MARCIE *gives the flyer to* JO.

MARCIE: He was a friend of Dean Olsen's. Well actually, Dean was one of Rocco's associates.

JO: So the cheque to Ruben was ...?

MARCIE: A loan. A loan he couldn't repay. And Rocco was about to – Give that to me.

> MARCIE *looks at the flyer. Punches in a number she sees on it into her phone.*

JO: Be careful, Mum.

MARCIE: No time for that now, honey. We're too close. (*on the phone*) Yeah. Can I talk to Rocco? ... No, that's okay. Just tell him that Ruben Joseph is standing across the street from 96 Willowbank ... No, he's not dead. That was Dean's body in the club. Tell Rocco he's getting fucked ... Yeah. Willowbank. Ninety-six. (*disconnecting*) Okay then ...

AMIE: What now?

MARCIE: Now we wait.

> *MARCIE's phone goes off. She answers it.*

MARCIE: (*on the phone*) Hold your horses, Ruben. We're still thinking about how to give you what you need ... We *both* know what it is.

> *MARCIE disconnects.*

MARCIE: If this all works out ... Have you been thinking about how to get Suzy away from Jimmy?

JO: Yeah.

MARCIE: I figured.

AMIE: You told me he never leaves you alone with her.

JO: He doesn't. But I know how to distract him long enough for one of you to take her.

MARCIE: Just don't do anything you'll have to go to a doctor for later.

> *MARCIE picks up a canvas bag from the floor beside the couch, and takes out her knitting.*

JO: What are you doing?

MARCIE: I've been trying to finish these socks for Suzy for quite a while now.

JO: And now is as good a time as any, eh? (*to AMIE*) Are you seeing this?

AMIE: (*chewing on a pickle*) Everyone has their own way of dealing with stress. I eat. A lot.

MARCIE: Well, youse never know it.

AMIE: You burn a lot of calories working that pole.

MARCIE: Which reminds me... (*to JO*) Have you had any thoughts yet about a new profession?

JO: No.

MARCIE: Why not?

JO: It might be because I've been kinda worried about someone bursting through our door and blowing all our heads off.

MARCIE: That was never going to happen.

JO: You're sure of that, are you?

MARCIE: Well, I've never felt threatened like that.

AMIE: I have.

MARCIE: Well, maybe I'm just used to people trying to get things from me. (*off JO*) Her father wanted to be waited on hand and foot. In all my retail jobs, I was expected to take immense amounts of shit from the customers. And now I've got these credit card companies asking me to pay 30 percent on my overdue account. So these guys are just –

JO: Different. These guys are different. I thought you would have figured that out by now.

AMIE: Yeah, me too.

MARCIE: Well, I've never worked in an "exotic" club, so I've never experienced the charms of men like this before. (*holding up a knitted sock*) Do you think she'll like them?

JO: Yeah...

AMIE: They're pretty. (*to MARCIE*) Do you think you can teach me how to knit sometime?

49

JO: Of course she can. She'll just start hanging in your bakery and when you have a few extra minutes –

Suddenly from outside: the sound of a car screeching to a halt and male voices yelling. JO goes to the window.

MARCIE: What's happening, honey?

JO: Some guys are grabbing Ruben ... and throwing him into their car and ...

The sound of a car speeding away.

JO: ... taking the fuck off. Oh. And here comes Rick from around the back of the building. He looks at the car speeding away. Pauses to let what's happened sink into his stupid head ... and ... runs like hell in the opposite direction.

MARCIE: Like I said, very efficient.

JO: Who?

MARCIE: Haven't you been paying attention? Rocco.

JO: Jesus ...

AMIE: Poor Rick. He was in way over his head with this stuff.

JO: This stuff being ...?

AMIE: Well, obviously, him and Ruben killed Dean Olsen, then burned the club down around him.

MARCIE: Good girl. And they killed the owners too. Those brothers.

JO: Wow, okay ... I was screwing a fucking murderer. I think I need a moment to – The Rileys? Why them too?

MARCIE: Well, it would look suspicious if they found just one body. And it wasn't one of the owners. I mean –

AMIE: Why would Dean be there alone? Right.

MARCIE: Well, yeah...

JO: (*in a bit of a daze*) Yeah... couldn't be alone... Had to kill all three. Kill all... Jesus... (*to* AMIE) So when Rick was inside you it probably didn't feel any different than some other guy, right? Same as me with Ruben. Just another dick. Except now I'm wondering... because it was actually a killer's dick, was there actually something I should have...

MARCIE's phone goes off.

MARCIE: (*on the phone*) Hey there... Yeah, it was pretty smooth... So where does that leave us?... Are you serious?... Well, that's very generous...

JO: Rocco?

MARCIE nods.

MARCIE: (*on the phone*) And you're really okay with that?... Wow. That's great... Yeah these last few years have been pretty rough, alright... No worries. We're on our way out of this place. You'll never hear from us again, promise... Yeah, to you too.

MARCIE disconnects, goes into the kitchen.

AMIE: What's she doing?

JO: Beats me.

MARCIE brings out three cans of beer.

MARCIE: (*handing one to each of them*) I've been saving these for a special occasion... (*to* JO) Right?

JO: Yeah...

AMIE: Beer? Beer for a special occasion?

MARCIE: They're imported. Crack 'em open, girls. We've been given a green light.

JO: To do what?

MARCIE: Anything we want. Anything we can do with $300,000. Rocco has set us free, bless him. The only man who has ever treated me with any degree of understanding is a hardcore criminal. Yes, he had me beaten a little, but when the story got told he –

JO: Mum.

MARCIE: We can cash the cheque. The money is actually his because Dean Olsen was working for him when he gave Ruben that loan. But he doesn't need it back.

JO: Because?

MARCIE: Rocco had taken out huge life insurance policies on all his "associates," probably because the nature of their work carried with it a certain amount of risk. Dean's was worth five million, so –

JO: Jesus…

MARCIE: Yes. So now, because of me, they can prove he's dead. At least, once they convince Ruben to –

AMIE: Confess…

MARCIE: Right. And because Rocco knows how desperate I must have been to go to him in the first place –

JO: He's opened up his gangster's heart to you and given you all that money.

MARCIE: As long as we keep it to ourselves. I mean, he has a rep to think about. (*to* JO) I told you it was meant to be.

JO: You told me it was from God. Not a vicious loan shark.

MARCIE: Well, I'm no expert on God, but apparently He works in myst–

JO: Please.

MARCIE: Okay, think what you want. But in the meantime, drink up. Then we've got some serious planning to do. (*downing her whole can*) This time I'm going to make it all the way.

AMIE: To the bank.

MARCIE: Right. I won't be long.

MARCIE leaves.

AMIE: I'm a little numb.

JO: Yeah. She does her best work when she gets other people a little numb.

JO has fetched a mostly full bottle of whisky from the kitchen.

AMIE: That your mum's stash?

JO: We share it.

JO takes a fairly long drink.

AMIE: I'm numb. And excited. I'm not kidding about baking things.

AMIE takes the bottle and drinks.

JO: I know.

AMIE: Ever since I was a little girl –

JO: I know.

AMIE: And now we have to concentrate on what you want.

JO: I want my daughter.

AMIE: Right.

JO: It won't matter what job I wind up in as long as I have her with me.

AMIE: I know. But it'd be nice if you were doing something you enjoyed. Remember all that drawing you did when we were in grade school. Those drawings were beautiful.

JO: (*taking a drink*) They were cartoons.

AMIE: Beautiful cartoons. And maybe you could –

JO: Do it, like, professionally? Come on.

AMIE: Why not?

JO: Amie. I don't have a dream about that stuff. I never did. I never wanted to be this or that. I sometimes thought about having babies, but that's all I ever –

AMIE: (*taking a drink*) Everyone has dreams. All the other girls at the club had dreams.

JO: They were all idiots.

AMIE: Emily wasn't. She was going to law school.

JO: She dropped out.

AMIE: What? No, she didn't.

JO: Yeah. A year ago. (*taking a drink*) She told me one night when we were both high.

AMIE: Why? (*taking a drink*) Why'd she drop out?

JO: She couldn't hack it, why else?

AMIE: So, why didn't she tell the rest of us?

JO: She asked me not to.

AMIE: Yeah, I get that. As long as we all thought she was heading towards something, it was like her dream was still alive. It meant to us it was alive.

JO: So, you were keeping her dream *alive* for her when all *she* wanted was to make money, get high, and party?

AMIE: I looked up to her.

JO: Yeah, well, that's what she wanted, wasn't it?

They pass the bottle back and forth twice quickly.

AMIE: Do you think you'll really be able to leave this life?

JO: Yeah.

AMIE: I mean, right now? Like, today?

JO: Why not today? The club's gone. And you have to stop sometime, right? I'm not up for a boob job every second year.

AMIE: Me neither. But ...

JO: What?

AMIE: I'll miss some things.

They can hold their liquor but they're both feeling it a little.

JO: You mean the men? The regulars who came there just for you? You'll miss all that attention?

AMIE: I guess. Maybe.

JO: You could probably hang in for a few more years.

AMIE: If I go under the knife ...

JO: Yeah, well, they're getting younger all the time. And the new ones won't need any cosmetic help for a while, so –

AMIE: I've learned a few tricks that'd keep me in demand for the private stuff.

JO: Yeah. Remember when we agreed not to talk about what goes on in those rooms? Let's not start now, okay?

AMIE: I just –

JO: (*taking a drink*) No. We're still two friends who met in that sandbox. I'd like to hold on to that, okay? You know, thinking it's the most important thing we share.

AMIE: So you're, what, ashamed?

JO: No. I'm just –

AMIE: It sounds like you are.

JO: No. Not ashamed. But Jesus, what's it add up to beyond the money? Money I already threw away.

AMIE: Because you were ashamed?

JO: No! Because I got addicted. To the drugs, the "social life," all the bullshit attention.

AMIE: Well, at least we never did porn.

JO: I wish I had. All that stuff we were acting onstage. At least porn would have been closer to the real thing.

AMIE: Depends on who you were fucking. They hire those guys for their cocks, not their faces. And definitely not for their personalities.

JO: But at least you'd be actually fucking. Not just...

AMIE: Teasing...

JO: Yeah. Like anyone with half a brain couldn't figure out that it was all fake.

AMIE: Yeah. (*drinking*) So... you're really thinking about moving on, then?

JO: Yeah. And so are you, right? Right?

AMIE: Yeah. But I'm holding on to the possibility of failure.

JO: The failure to move on?

AMIE: No. To move but to then fail.

JO: At baking?

AMIE: Or anything.

JO: Okay. But don't tell my mum that. Because she'll be all over you. She wants us all to be betting on success.

AMIE: What?

JO: She saw some guy on TV saying that a few months ago. "Bet on success and you can't go wrong." I'm pretty sure she blames all her money problems on always betting on failure. Like her mother did. And probably her grandmother did too. They couldn't help it. Brought up poor, that's how you roll, right?

AMIE: For sure.

JO: Anyway, that's why I knew when she found that cheque we were in for a wild ride. Finally a chance to bet on success. So if you want a little peace and quiet you better get on board.

AMIE: Yeah. I'll try.

JO: Okay... something else. I don't wanna have to bang Jimmy to get Suzy away from him, so we need to come up with something that puts him out of commission.

AMIE: Like poison maybe?

JO: Or maybe not that extreme.

AMIE: Like a roofy?

JO: Sure, that could work. You can come on to him and –

AMIE: Me? Why me?

JO: Because it wouldn't work with me. He knows I hate his guts. But he thinks you've secretly had the hots for him all these years.

AMIE: No way.

JO: The guy thinks he's a gift to all women. Look, all you have to do is show up, make sure Suzy goes to her room, and then come on to him.

AMIE: Fucking yuk.

JO: And then slip it into his drink.

AMIE: I can't let him touch me.

JO: You'll have to let him do something to get him going.

AMIE: Okay. Okay, he can touch me. But not down there. He can have a little boob play.

JO: That should be enough. Then when he's out, you call, I come in, we grab Suzy and anything she wants to take with her.

AMIE: Bobby Bunny, probably.

JO: Right. We gotta get Bobby B. Or she'll go nuts... And then we're gone... Okay?

AMIE: Yeah. Unless I can come up with a better idea.

MARCIE comes back in.

MARCIE: All good. They asked a couple of questions like they're supposed to, I guess. I told them they weren't entitled to know anything about where I got it because it wasn't cash.

JO: Is that true?

MARCIE: It seemed to be. They called Dean Olsen's bank to find out if the cheque would be covered, and...

AMIE: No problem?

MARCIE: No. (*to JO*) They put it in our account.

MARCIE produces a receipt.

JO: *Our* account?

MARCIE: Yeah, the one we opened to put the rent in. I had high hopes for us then.

AMIE: Meaning?

MARCIE: That we had a common purpose.

JO: She hoped that I'd be contributing.

MARCIE: Well, you got sidetracked.

JO: Yeah. That's one word for it.

AMIE: It's a good enough word. People can get really fucking sidetracked sometimes. Booze, the wrong drugs, really bad men. But we're past that now, right?

MARCIE: Speaking of booze. (*off the bottle*) That was nearly full.

AMIE: We were having a serious, no-bullshit discussion.

JO: And we needed to take the edge off. (*to AMIE*) At least that's what I think.

AMIE: And you're right.

JO: And... it worked.

MARCIE: Yeah, I can tell.

JO: No, you can't.

AMIE: She means we can hold our liquor so –

JO: No, you fucking can't tell.

AMIE: Anyway. Here's the receipt. (*handing it to JO*) Amazing, eh? Can't be many people who had their bank balance go from forty-three to three hundred thousand and forty-three with one deposit. Like I said, a miracle.

JO: You said a gift from God.

MARCIE: And that's not a miracle?

JO: I'm just wondering if God's gonna help out all the other people with just forty-three dollars or less in the bank.

MARCIE: Okay. I get that. (*taking out her phone*) No more God talk.

JO: Who are you calling now?

MARCIE: I'm going to make a reservation at a fancy restaurant for the three of us. We need to celebrate. (*looking at them*) Any ideas?

> *JO and AMIE look at each other. JO shrugs.*

AMIE: Rick took me somewhere once. He was trying to impress me.

MARCIE: What was it called?

AMIE: It didn't have a name.

MARCIE: It had to have a name.

AMIE: Not anywhere I could find it. Not on the door, not on the menus. Rick just called it... a place.

MARCIE: A place.

AMIE: Yeah... Maybe *that's* its name. (*to JO*) Google it.

> *JO does.*

AMIE: Couldn't we just go out for a burger?

MARCIE: On the best night of our lives? Absolutely not.

JO: Yeah, here it is. "A Place." It's on Hoskins.

MARCIE: (*to JO*) And it was swanky?

JO: Yeah. He dropped a bundle.

MARCIE: Then that's where we're going. (*to JO*) What's their number?

JO: There isn't one. Says they don't accept reservations.

AMIE: Yeah, that's right. You just show up and if they like the look of you, they let you in.

MARCIE: What's up with that?

JO: It's just bullshit. We drop a hundred at the door, and we'll get in, no problem. But really... I think we should just go for Chalet Chicken or something.

AMIE: Oh yeah!

AMIE and JO: Chalet Chicken! Yay!

AMIE: Come on, Marcie. She's right. You wouldn't like it there. The food's okay, but it's mostly for rich –

JO: Assholes and crooks?

AMIE: We can still dress up, if you want.

MARCIE: For Chalet Chicken? We don't have to be stupid about it. I don't have something good to wear anyway. (*a little stagger*) Ohhh... I'm a little dizzy. (*heading for couch*) Better sit down...

JO: You okay?

MARCIE: (*sitting*) I think I've been letting myself get too worked up. (*to AMIE*) Pass me my knitting, will you?

AMIE: It's right beside you.

MARCIE: Oh good... (*picking it up*) Yeah, that was all just about... too much excitement... (*taking a deep breath*) You know what it's like, what just happened to us? It's like that movie where the guy shares his lottery winnings with a waitress.

JO: It's nothing like that.

MARCIE: Well, it was unexpected, right? Just like it was for her. Unexpected like so many things in life. Except this time it was actually good.

> *MARCIE takes a few deep breaths.*

JO: What are you doing?

MARCIE: Just trying to calm down ... So have you two made any decisions about where we should go?

AMIE: Not yet.

MARCIE: I was thinking maybe we should buy a car. Travel around a bit. Find some small town that suits our purpose.

JO: (*to AMIE*) Somewhere with no pastry shop.

AMIE: Yeah ... but a place that has a girls' hockey team.

MARCIE: Suzy wants to play hockey?

JO: Only if she can be the goalie.

AMIE: Tell her why?

JO: (*to MARCIE*) At the end of the game, when the teams line up to shake hands ... the goalie is always first in line.

MARCIE: And that's important to her?

JO: Go figure.

MARCIE: Well, I think it's a good sign. It shows a generosity of spirit.

JO: I think she just likes to be first.

MARCIE's phone goes off.

JO: What now?

MARCIE: (*looking at her phone's screen*) No, its okay ... (*on the phone*) Hi April ... No, it's good that you called. I can pay my bill off today. The whole thing ... Some money from Sheila's estate came in ... No, it was a surprise ... Yeah, great. So ... I'll drop in later with the money. And April, thanks for your patience. You've been very kind ... Okay. Bye.

AMIE: Who's April?

JO: She owns the little grocery around the corner.

MARCIE: She's been carrying us for six months.

MARCIE's phone goes off once more.

MARCIE: (*on the phone*) Speaking... Yes. Yes, I know it's way past due. But I'll be able to get it to you tomorrow... All of it... Okay, there's no need to be sarcastic... Well, if saying "whoopee" wasn't sarcastic, what was it then?... Oh, you're just really happy for me. Right. After three months of talking to me like I'm a criminal, all of a sudden you care.

JO: Tell him to fuck off.

MARCIE: It's a her.

AMIE: Bitch!

MARCIE: (*on the phone*) Look, there's something I've wanted to ask you for a while now. Do you own stocks in that bank?... No? Then why have you taken this whole thing so fucking personally?!

MARCIE disconnects. Another call comes in.

JO: Mum. Don't, okay?

MARCIE: It's my dentist's office. I should let them know the bill's going to get paid. Even though some of his work has been pretty shoddy lately.

JO: (*to AMIE*) She thinks he might be going blind. He's almost eighty.

MARCIE: Eighty-five.

AMIE: Jesus...

MARCIE: (*on the phone*) Hi, Celia. Guess what? You can tell him I'm going to pay it off tomorrow... Yes, all of it... You're welcome. Bye. (*disconnecting*) I don't think she believed me. I guess all those people I owe think I'm way beyond hope.

JO: Well, then they don't really know you, do they?

AMIE: (*to MARCIE*) Yeah. The way you worked this thing...

JO: You took on all those sleazy guys, and you got what you wanted.

AMIE: I was very impressed.

JO: Me too.

MARCIE: Really? Good. Because I think I might do something like this again. (*off their looks*) Not right away. But when we're settled somewhere else. If we ever need more cash. Or... if I just want to have a little fun.

JO and AMIE look at each other.

MARCIE: I wouldn't mind having more fun...

Blackout.

THE END

Claire Burns (Jo) in George F. Walker's *The Chance*, holding the three-hundred-thousand-dollar cheque.

Violet (Catherine Fitch), dragging an unconscious Leo (Tony Munch) in *Her Inside Life* at the Assembly Theatre in Toronto, Ontario (October 27 to November 18, 2018).

HER INSIDE LIFE

PRODUCTION HISTORY

Her Inside Life was first produced by Low Rise Productions at the Assembly Theatre in Toronto, Ontario, Canada, from October 27 to November 18, 2018. It played as a double bill with *Kill the Poor*, produced by Leroy Street Theatre. The cast and crew were as follows:

VIOLET	Catherine Fitch
CATHY	Sarah Murphy-Dyson
MADDY	Lesley Robertson
LEO	Tony Munch

Director	Andrea Wasserman
Stage Manager	Jenna Borsato
Set Designer	Chris Bretecher
Lighting Designer	Chin Palipane
Sound Designer	Jeremy Hutton and Will Jarvis
Costume Designer	Kathleen Black
Graphics Designer	Fook Communications
Photographer	John Gundy

SETTING

A low-income five-storey apartment building.

CHARACTERS

VIOLET, early fifties
CATHY, late thirties
MADDY, late twenties, Violet's daughter
LEO, late forties, Violet's brother-in-law

SCENE 1

A small two-bedroom apartment. Simply furnished. Reasonably tidy.

In the darkness we hear the building's fire alarm and several sirens down on the street.

VIOLET, in her early fifties, is sitting on her couch and seems to be trying to block out the sound by humming to herself, in tune with the sirens.

Suddenly she stands, goes into the kitchen, checks all the burners and the oven. Nothing's on.

She returns to the couch, sits, stands again, then returns to the kitchen and checks the oven and burners again. Still nothing wrong. She returns to the couch.

A knock on the door. She ignores it. Another knock, louder. She tries to ignore this one, too, but it's harder.

CATHY: (*from the hall*) Violet! (*knocking*) Violet!... (*knocking*) Vi! Open the door! You have to let me in. There's a fire in the building. You have to leave. Did you hear me?! There's a fire!

VIOLET: (*to herself*) Well, it's not in here. (*to Cathy*) I checked my stove! It's fine!

CATHY: (*off*) Let me in!

VIOLET: No. Go away. You're making me nervous.

CATHY: (*off*) I mean it, Vi. If you don't let me in, you're not going to be allowed to stay here.

VIOLET: You mean while the fire is still going?

CATHY: (*off*) I mean ever. You'll have to go back to the hospital.

VIOLET: That's out of the question.

CATHY: (*off*) No! It's not. Now let me in.

VIOLET: Okay, but you'll have to calm down a little. Like I said, you're making me nervous.

CATHY: (*off*) Jesus. There's a fire in the building, Violet!!

VIOLET: Okay. But how is getting so upset about it going to help?

CATHY: (*more calmly*) Vi. Please. Will you please just let me in?

VIOLET: Well, there you go. (*starting to the door*) Just asking nicely changes the whole situation.

> *VIOLET unlocks and opens the door. CATHY, in her late thirties, enters and follows VIOLET back to her couch.*

CATHY: Vi. What are you ...?

> *VIOLET sits down.*

CATHY: No, no, don't do that. We have to leave. They're evacuating the building.

VIOLET: Why?

CATHY: Because there's a fire!

VIOLET: Well, that's not my fault. Check the stove yourself if you don't believe me.

CATHY: Violet. Please listen to me.

VIOLET: I am. I am listening to you.

> *The sirens stop.*

VIOLET: Well, there you go. It's all over, whatever it was. You can leave now.

CATHY: Did you take your medication this morning?

VIOLET: Of course.

CATHY: Are you sure?

VIOLET: Absolutely.

CATHY: Can I see the pill bottle?

VIOLET: Why? Do you think I'm lying?

CATHY: No, I think you might be mistaken.

VIOLET: Well, even if I am, how could you tell?

CATHY: You mean other than from your behaviour?

VIOLET: Whatever that means. It's not like you count the pills, is it? Or do you? Do you come here every day and count my pills?

CATHY heads for the bathroom.

VIOLET: It's not in there.

Sounds of CATHY going through the medicine chest.

VIOLET: I said, it's not in there!

CATHY comes out of the bathroom.

CATHY: So where is it then?

VIOLET: I'm not sure. But it's definitely not in the bathroom. I keep it separate.

CATHY: Separate from what?

VIOLET: From all the things that *don't* hurt me.

CATHY: Your medication doesn't hurt you.

VIOLET: That's what you think, is it? Do you want to try it sometime?

CATHY: Tell me where your medication is, or I'm taking you back to the hospital.

VIOLET: You'll have to say that again. You didn't phrase it right.

CATHY: Sorry?

VIOLET: You're not supposed to say things that imply that you have control over me. Instead of saying "I'm taking you," you should have said "We're going" ... You know, like it's my idea, too. You're supposed to know better, Cathy. You're not all that new at this.

CATHY: No. I'm not. And you're right. So tell me where you keep your medication, or *we're* going back to the hospital.

VIOLET: On whose authority?

CATHY: Mine.

VIOLET: There you go again. We both know you can't initiate that action without getting authorization from your superiors.

CATHY: And who are they?

VIOLET: That team of doctors who've been running my life for several years now.

CATHY: They're not my superiors. We're a team.

VIOLET: Sure you are. You know, Cathy, sometimes you talk to me like you think I'm not very smart.

CATHY: I know you're smart, Vi. Believe me.

VIOLET: I taught school for twenty years. English literature. Dickens. Shakespeare. Ask me any question you want about the works of Jane Austen.

CATHY: You're not going to distract me, Vi. Making sure you take your medication is an important part of my job so –

VIOLET: Still on about that, are you?

CATHY: (*sitting next to her*) Have you stopped taking it all together? Or have you just cut back? (*off her blank stare*) Violet?

VIOLET: Cut back.

CATHY: To what? Every second day?

VIOLET: Something like that.

CATHY: Meaning?

VIOLET: Occasionally.

CATHY: (*exasperated now*) Which is?

VIOLET: When I think I need it, okay? I take a goddamn pill when I think I need one.

CATHY: And what determines that? What is it that makes you think it might be a good idea for you to take one of your pills?

VIOLET: When I think I might be losing touch with reality.

CATHY: Okay. Give me an example of when that happened.

VIOLET: I can't remember one at the moment. It hasn't happened for a while.

CATHY: It just did. Sirens were blaring down on the street. The building's fire alarm was going off. And you just checked your stove.

VIOLET: What else should I have done?

CATHY: Remember all those safety procedures we went over when I first moved you in?

VIOLET: You mean when you *helped* me move in.

CATHY: Yes. Sorry. When I helped you move in, we went through a list of things to do when the fire alarm sounds. The first and most important one is that you go to a stairwell and... get the hell out of the building!

VIOLET: Shhh. Too much. Too upset. Too loud.

CATHY: You're right. Sorry. But do you remember me telling you that? If the fire alarm goes off, you leave.

VIOLET: Yes. I do remember. I know I should do that. But I have ... I have ...

CATHY: You have what?

VIOLET: Well, you're the expert, so you know what I have. Or hasn't this come up?

CATHY: Hasn't what come up?

VIOLET: The problem I have with leaving the building.

CATHY: You're always allowed to leave it if it's on fire.

VIOLET: That's not the problem I'm referring to. I'm talking about the problem I've developed recently with it.

CATHY: How recently?

VIOLET: Well, a few minutes ago apparently. I mean leaving the *apartment* is hard enough. Just getting to the garbage chute ... But when I heard all that noise –

CATHY: That noise being the alarm and the sirens.

VIOLET: Which was still noise, so I don't understand your need to interrupt me just so you could say that again.

CATHY: Okay. I get that. So you heard all that ... noise and ...

VIOLET: And I knew I'd be required to leave the building. That's when it hit me that I had a serious issue with doing that.

CATHY: Okay.

VIOLET: Which I suppose is something else we have to "deal" with now.

CATHY: Yes. Right. But in the meantime you can probably deal with it yourself.

VIOLET: Myself? Really?

CATHY: To some extent, yes. With some help from your meds.

VIOLET: Well, that's new. Are you saying I won't have to have a meeting with my doctors for a re-evaluation?

CATHY: I'm saying it will be easier if you're on your meds. And I'm also saying that even if it isn't easier or easy *enough*, it's still something you *have* to make yourself overcome in an emergency.

VIOLET: Wow. Well, as they used to say on the commune, "That's some heavy shit."

CATHY: What commune? When were you were on a commune? In your teens? For how long?

VIOLET: Long enough to experience some of the things being offered in an alternative lifestyle.

CATHY: What's that mean? Did you take drugs when you were there? Did you ever take LSD, Violet? Because there are numerous studies tying schizophrenia to –

VIOLET: Relax. I was messing with you. I've never been anywhere near a commune. And by the way, doctors have been asking me for years if I ever took LSD. So I know all about those "studies." Kettle's boiling.

VIOLET starts back to the kitchen.

CATHY: I need a key to your apartment.

VIOLET: (*from the kitchen*) No you don't.

VIOLET finds the kettle off.

CATHY: If you're going to stay here, yes I do. I want you to give me a key, so I can get a copy made.

VIOLET: How about if I promise to leave every time that stupid alarm goes off... (*exiting kitchen*) ... which is sometimes five times a day because a few of the teenagers in here are thoughtless idiots.

CATHY: People do.

VIOLET: People do what?

CATHY: They leave. When they hear the alarm and the fire engines, they leave the building.

VIOLET: Every time?

CATHY: Jesus weeps. Yes! Every time.

VIOLET: (*shrugging*) Okay. If that's the way they choose to lead their lives, but I –

CATHY: I'm getting your key copied.

VIOLET: I think that's a contravention of my legal and constitutional rights.

CATHY: It's not actually. You have almost no rights now.

VIOLET: How can that be true?

CATHY: We've been over this several times. The court found you not criminally responsible but also still a potential danger to society. And that means –

VIOLET: I've got you in my life forever.

CATHY: It ... means you are to be monitored closely, and you are required to be on medication until such time as you are –

VIOLET: Dead.

CATHY: No. Ready.

VIOLET: Ready to die.

CATHY: No, ready ... and capable of showing us that –

VIOLET: I can make my own decisions? But I can't, can I? Not really. I can't be who I want to be. Live where I want to live. Decide not to put certain substances into my body. None of those things. And all because of what? Something I've done in the past.

CATHY: And you know what that was, don't you? You haven't forgotten.

VIOLET: Of course not. And I had very good reasons for taking that action, as you well know. Reasons that were never given the weight they deserved by your precious court.

CATHY: I know you think that but –

VIOLET: Well, would you kill *your* husband and *your* brother-in-law without having a reason to justify what you'd done?

CATHY: I need your key.

They look at each other.

CATHY: I mean it, Vi. I need it.

VIOLET: Okay...

VIOLET takes a key on a chain from around her neck and hands it to CATHY.

CATHY: Just promise me you won't abuse the privilege.

CATHY smiles, then leaves. VIOLET seems very worried. She starts to move in a circle.

Blackout.

SCENE 2

VIOLET's daughter MADDY, in her late twenties,
is looking around the apartment. VIOLET is in
the kitchen.

VIOLET: (*from the kitchen*) I control what I can control.
I control my stove, so I won't start a fire in here. (*exiting the*
kitchen with a spray cleaner and a sponge) I control the water
temperature in my shower so I don't scald myself. I check
my thermostat to maintain a moderate temperature in my
environment at all times. If I spill a substance on the floor,
I clean it up so I don't slip, fall, and break a bone. (*returning*
to the kitchen) What happens outside my living area I have no
control over, so I try not to worry about it. There are people
outside my living area who do dangerous things. There are
people out in the world who are harming us in ways we can't
even fathom. (*exiting the kitchen*) I've tried in the past to fight
against those people and those things, but that caused me
great pain and uncertainty and also a loss of my freedom. So I
checked my stove and I think that should be the end of my
responsibilities in that matter.

MADDY: Are you eating?

VIOLET: No, I'm cleaning.

MADDY: I mean, when you eat ... do you eat well?

VIOLET: (*from the kitchen*) Are you asking if I eat salads? (*exiting*
the kitchen) Why would I start now? You know, some people
think that salads are only suitable for cows. Creatures that have
four stomachs. Because you need at least four stomachs to
digest that stuff properly. Just like you'd need for grass.

MADDY: Mum?

VIOLET: Yes, darling?

MADDY: Knock it off. Just tell me what you eat, okay?

VIOLET: I'll make you a list if it makes you feel better. A list of all the food I eat. Plus whatever garbage has been added to that food. Everything that I consume and how often I consume it.

MADDY: I'm just worried about you.

VIOLET: Are you? Well, maybe you could find another way to show it besides talking to me like I'm a child.

> VIOLET *comes out of the kitchen with a plate of Oreo cookies. Stacked very high.*

MADDY: What's that?

VIOLET: Lunch.

MADDY: Okay. Good.

> MADDY *picks up a cookie.*

VIOLET: Oreos. Lunch is just Oreos.

MADDY: Right. My favourite.

> MADDY *bites into a cookie.*

MADDY: Mum?

VIOLET: What?

MADDY: Aren't you going to join me for lunch?

VIOLET: No.

MADDY: Why not?

VIOLET: (*grabbing the plate of cookies*) Because it was a joke for Chrissake! And you know that, so why did you have to ruin it?

> *She takes the Oreos back to the kitchen.*

VIOLET: As if, even on my worst day, I'd serve my daughter a plate of Oreo cookies for lunch. I was just trying to scare you into thinking I'd totally lost it.

MADDY: So it wasn't actually a joke then?

VIOLET: Well, it would have been if you'd laughed.

MADDY: The last time I was here you made me a grilled cheese sandwich without any cheese in it. Was that a joke too?

VIOLET: Might have been. Is that why you disappeared for all that time? You didn't like me making jokes about my possible –

MADDY: I didn't disappear. I just needed a –

VIOLET: You disappeared from my life. That's my point. Okay, you don't want to talk about it. So let's get back to the most important thing.

MADDY: And what's that?

VIOLET: My sense of humour. You know, a fairly severe bipolar disorder, or even schizophrenia, or whatever it is I'm supposed to have, does not vanquish a person's sense of humour. I mean, not necessarily. Or not entirely. In fact, it can even enhance it. I could make you some soup, but it will have to be out of a can. I can only offer you what's brought to me by my "psychiatric" social worker. She's not much on nutrition for some reason, and I'm not allowed to go shopping.

MADDY: Not allowed by whom?

VIOLET: Myself mostly. I don't trust my ability to cope in the stressful environment of a supermarket. I seem to remember that you have a similar problem.

MADDY: I got over it.

VIOLET: Really? How?

MADDY: I only go shopping when I'm drunk now.

VIOLET: Was that a joke?

MADDY: Yeah.

VIOLET: Well it wasn't funny.

MADDY: Okay. So now you know how it feels. How about that smaller store near here?

VIOLET: Oh no. I tried going there when I first moved in. It's run by an older Korean woman.

MADDY: You don't like Koreans?

VIOLET: I love Koreans. My favourite student was Korean. It's just that the woman in the store didn't understand my questions.

MADDY: Well maybe next time don't ask her any.

VIOLET: My questions weren't frivolous, Maddy. I didn't know where all the items I needed were.

MADDY: It's a very small store, Mum. Maybe next time just look a little harder.

VIOLET: And if that doesn't work? You see my point? Shopping, no matter where you do it, can be very unsettling.

MADDY: Not if you keep a flask of vodka in your bag.

VIOLET: I'm starting to think you're not joking about that at all.

MADDY: It's okay, Mum. I go to meetings, I've got a sponsor. I've got it under control.

VIOLET: Are you sure about that, honey?

MADDY: No. But here's the thing. I don't know if I can ever actually be honest with you. You know, tell you about what's really going on with me like I used to ... and not always treat you like you're ...

VIOLET: Crazy.

MADDY: Sensitive.

VIOLET: Sensitive to the point of being crazy. Anyway, we're working on that. My sensitivity. My shopping anxiety ...

not allowing myself to leave the apartment. Cathy and I have plans.

MADDY: What kind of plans?

VIOLET: Big ones. Well, hers are big. Mine are more modest. It all comes down to proper management of my medication. Too much and I might as well be in a coma. Too little and, well, things get ...

MADDY: Dangerous?

VIOLET: Adventurous. How are the kids?

MADDY: They're good.

VIOLET: Can you bring them by sometime?

MADDY: We're talking about that.

VIOLET: Yes, of course. Dennis should have a say.

MADDY: Right. But I meant Cathy and I are talking about it.

VIOLET: Cathy has a say about whether or not I can see my grandchildren?

MADDY: Yeah. She does, Mum. I think you know that.

VIOLET: Sure. Well, she certainly has her hand firmly on every part of my existence, doesn't she? So, how far along are you and Cathy in terms of making that decision?

MADDY: I'm not sure. The kids want to see you, so that's not an issue.

VIOLET: I miss them. It breaks my heart not seeing them. I could show you what it's doing to me, you know. I'm holding myself together right now because I don't want to scare you by demonstrating how it's actually affecting me.

MADDY: I know how it's affecting you, Mum!

VIOLET: Oh you think so, do you? (*pulling a handful of hair from her head*) Look at this! This is a symptom of heartbreak and disappointment!!

She reaches for her hair again. MADDY *grabs her arm.*

MADDY: Mum! Please! I get it!

VIOLET: Good.

They look at each other.

VIOLET: That's good…

MADDY: Yeah. But we can't just ignore what Cathy –

VIOLET: How does Dennis feel about it?

MADDY: Dennis…?

VIOLET: Your husband.

MADDY: Yeah… Well he's for it, I think. But he's not really good at making these kinds of decisions so –

VIOLET: Don't disparage him now! I know you can't help yourself, but it's not good for me to hear how bitter you've become about him.

MADDY: I was only trying to tell you that he sometimes can't –

VIOLET: I love him! I love the kind of father he's become. Especially considering his dismal family background. And I love that he supports your career even when you're not fully applying yourself.

MADDY: Yeah, he's been very –

VIOLET: Kind. He's an exceptionally kind person.

MADDY: Right. He's a saint! It's a wonder he puts up with me! I mean, I can barely put up with myself, so –

VIOLET: If your father had been one tenth as kind as Dennis, he might still be alive today!

MADDY: Mum. Please don't start.

VIOLET: I'm just saying that the man had many flaws. He was deceitful, greedy, and kind of stupid. But it was his inability to show any degree of kindness towards other people that did him in. (*looking at her*) So it's really up to Cathy then. If she's okay with it, I get to see my grandchildren.

MADDY: Yeah. But I don't think she's totally against it. She's just –

VIOLET: Cautious. Very cautious. And as personality traits go, that's not always bad. Not nearly so bad as impatience, which by the way was another of your father's flaws and probably the one that got him killed.

MADDY: Mum, this isn't going to help either of us.

VIOLET: Why not?

MADDY: Because it might not be –

VIOLET: Accurate? Oh right. Sorry. It was actually *my* impatience that doomed him. But you can only take hearing about and even witnessing so many of a person's misdeeds before you take action. Especially after you've tried to warn the authorities about him and they've ignored you, or even worse, blamed your "illness" for what you were telling them about a man who was so clearly a danger to society. And then later when your patience runs out and you're forced to take matters into your own hands, instead of investigating why you did what you did, they put you in front of a judge who condemns you to a life of supervision and constant medical intervention. Is that fair?

MADDY: You murdered him, Mum!

VIOLET: Well someone had to, honey. He was a serial killer!!

Blackout.

SCENE 3

MADDY is letting CATHY in. The shower is running.

MADDY: Thanks for coming so quickly.

CATHY: Well, you sounded pretty worried.

MADDY: I got scared.

CATHY: Because you think she's getting worse?

MADDY: Yeah. Or maybe ...

CATHY: What?

MADDY: Maybe it's me. It's like ... You know how at some point in your life you start seeing a lot of your parent in yourself?

CATHY: That's happening to you?

MADDY: Well, sometimes when she's saying things, I –

CATHY: She's ill.

MADDY: I know, but maybe I am too. Because when she's saying certain things it's like I hear myself talking and –

CATHY: You're not ill, Maddy. You're just overwhelmed.

MADDY: Ya think?

CATHY: Yeah, she can be a handful. I mean, some of the things that come out of her mouth ...

MADDY: The worst is when she seems to be making sense.

CATHY: Yeah, so what's that about?

MADDY: You're asking me?

CATHY: No, I'm just thinking out loud.

MADDY: I want to help her. I want her to get better. But mostly I just want her to stop scaring me. I think it might help if you let her see my kids.

CATHY: Help you?

MADDY: No. Help *her* ... to, you know, calm down a little. Well yeah, okay, it might help me, too. Because I feel pretty guilty about her not having any contact with them.

CATHY: She will as soon as we get her more stabilized.

MADDY: But how long is that going to take?

CATHY: Well first she'll have to start trusting that her doctors and I know more about her condition than she does.

MADDY: They miss her. Shawna especially.

CATHY: Sure. But if she's having a bad day she could scare them. Or even –

MADDY: She'd never hurt them.

CATHY: Not intentionally. But the psychotic break she had was so intense and so prolonged that we don't – When was the last time they saw her?

MADDY: Just after her hearing. She was in the hospital.

CATHY: And that went okay?

MADDY: There was a policeman outside her door. That kinda freaked them out.

CATHY: And how was *she*?

MADDY: She was excited to see them. She'd painted all her fingers.

CATHY: Sorry?

MADDY: For her puppet show.

CATHY: She did a puppet show for them ... with her fingers.

MADDY: Yeah, she used to do them for me.

CATHY: Okay. Were they fun?

MADDY: Never. And neither was this one. In it she was trying to explain to the children what went on with her and my dad. Their grandfather was the thumb, and he was a very large, angry man. And my mum was the pinky finger trying to stand up to him. I stopped it when I realized where it was going.

CATHY: The pinky finger about to kill the thumb.

MADDY: I don't know what it had in mind, but it was definitely getting pretty worked up. Shaking. Kind of twisting around...

MADDY demonstrates.

CATHY: Getting ready to attack...

MADDY: It was weird. But the kids didn't get any of it.

CATHY: Did they laugh? Tell me they fucking laughed.

MADDY: No. But they didn't run out of the room screaming, either, which is what *I* felt like doing. (*shrugging*) They just wanted to be with her, I think. They're kinda used to her behaviour. They were both born after she had to leave teaching.

CATHY: Have you ever talked to them about that, why she left?

MADDY: We've talked about burnout. And they've seen *me* after a bad shift at the restaurant.

CATHY: Not exactly the same thing.

MADDY: Close enough. Try making the chef's special crème brûlée while the asshat shouts in your ear, (*in a stereotypical Parisian French accent*) "Not like that, you idiot. It's slightly burned maybe here or there. Not the whole fucking thing!" ... I mean, that crap is a bitch to get right at the best of times but – There you go. That sounds like something she might say. Jesus. Okay. Tell me something now.

CATHY: Tell you what?

MADDY: Put it into some kind of ... context. Normalize it a bit. Help me stop feeling that she and I are locked away together in a very dark place.

CATHY: Well, first of all –

MADDY: I know. It's not me. It's just her. But it *feels* like it's the both of us.

CATHY: When you're with her.

MADDY: Well, she can be very unsettling.

CATHY: And funny. She can be very funny.

MADDY: Yeah, but the thing is I'm not sure she always knows when she's funny or when she's ...

MADDY and CATHY: Unsettling ...

CATHY: Plus. Your mother might be the extreme edge of a possible epidemic.

MADDY: An epidemic? Jesus. You mean there are a lot more of her out there?

CATHY: I see a lot of middle-aged women who seem to be on the verge of totally losing it. And I'm talking about women who didn't go through half of what your mother did with your father and everything he did or might have done. I mean, before she ...

MADDY: Blew his head off.

CATHY: When I hear some of those women talk about their lives, it's like they're just having a normal response to how they're being treated in the world. One woman thought her condition was caused by dusting.

MADDY: Dusting ...

CATHY: It took up way too much of her time. Especially (*in a strange whisper*) "Those goddamn book shelves!"

MADDY: Jesus...

CATHY: Yeah, Jesus... Okay look, here's the news of the day. I was going to call and give you a heads-up, but here I am so... Leo's out of prison.

MADDY: Why? For good behaviour?

CATHY: Maybe.

MADDY: He doesn't know where she is, does he?

CATHY: No, of course not. But I'm thinking I might tell her he's out. It could help her get some things straight.

MADDY: Well, I don't know if it'll help her, but it's definitely gonna shock her. She thinks she killed him.

CATHY: No. She just likes thinking that she did. It was important for her to believe that both your father and your uncle Leo were no longer walking among us.

MADDY: And now?

CATHY: You mean today? Who knows? But a few months ago, when we had her stabilized, she told me she figured it was actually only Keith who was the contract killer and that Leo just... helped him somehow. She still thought that Leo had to be made accountable but –

MADDY: So she suddenly remembered all this? Why wasn't I told?

CATHY: You couldn't be found. Even your husband didn't know where you were.

MADDY: Yeah. Maddy needed some serious Maddy time.

CATHY just looks at her.

CATHY: Anyway... she stayed on her meds long enough to connect to reality. It was a good sign.

MADDY: That she was getting better...

CATHY: She'll never get better, Maddy. But if we can keep her on her meds...

VIOLET comes out of the bathroom in a robe, post shower, her hair in a towel.

VIOLET: So have you decided anything?

MADDY: About what?

VIOLET: About me, honey. What else would you be talking about?

MADDY: Cathy thinks it's just a matter of time until we can bring Shawna and Kyle to see you.

VIOLET: Really? Well, isn't she a sweetheart.

CATHY: Did you enjoy your shower? You were in there for quite a while.

VIOLET: It's my favourite place on the planet. Why? Were you worried I was doing something drastic to myself?

CATHY: You're not self-destructive, Violet. We know that.

VIOLET: Do we?

CATHY: I meant my team and I. So you can stop trying to convince me otherwise. Come on over. We need to talk.

VIOLET: Oh. Well, talking would be wonderful. I've sincerely enjoyed the few occasions when we've actually done that. (*to* MADDY) What she *really* means is that she needs to *tell* me something. Tell me how to correct something in my behaviour. How to understand something about my situation. How to comply with my legal and medical obligations...

CATHY: Violet. Come. Sit.

VIOLET does.

VIOLET: (*smiling*) I'm all ears.

*CATHY and MADDY exchange a look. CATHY turns
and smiles at VIOLET.*

CATHY: Leo got out of prison yesterday.

VIOLET: (*smiling again*) Did he, now? So there's a prison for
corpses, is there?

MADDY: Mum.

VIOLET: I killed him. I shot them both in the head.

MADDY: You shot Dad in the head. You shot Uncle Leo in
the neck.

VIOLET: Close enough.

CATHY: Not really.

MADDY: He's alive.

CATHY: Which is something you already knew, Violet.

VIOLET: Okay. What else do I know?

CATHY: I'm sorry?

VIOLET: I mean, what else do I know that I've forgotten I know?

CATHY: Just that. He's alive. And I wanted you to know that he's
out of prison.

VIOLET: So that I can have him over for dinner?

CATHY: So that you'll know what's going on. What really is. And
what isn't.

VIOLET: Alright. But back to that dinner thing. (*to MADDY*)
Do you think that would be a good idea?

MADDY: Not really.

CATHY: (*to VIOLET*) Do *you*?

VIOLET: Well, I did try to kill him. So I guess I might owe him an apology. I seem to remember he liked beef stroganoff. Yes. I could make that! (*heading to the kitchen*) I've got a great recipe somewhere.

MADDY: (*quietly, to* CATHY) What's she doing?

CATHY: Looking for the recipe.

MADDY: I mean, do you think she believes you about Leo being alive?

CATHY: Let's assume she does and take it from there.

VIOLET comes back into the room.

VIOLET: (*coming back carrying a meat cleaver*) Couldn't find the recipe. But I found this instead. Is it okay if I don't cook for him and I just finish the job this time?

She mimes cutting off a head then holding it up.

MADDY: I think it's just a joke...

CATHY just sighs.

Blackout.

SCENE 4

VIOLET is setting the table for two and suppressing a giggle.

VIOLET: (*talking to the other place setting*) What a harrowing story. And you're not even a homosexual as far as I know. I mean, if you were, then all that sodomy that was committed on you in prison might have been, at least potentially, enjoyable. Not that gay men enjoy being raped. No one enjoys being raped. I think I just got confused about that. It's actually me. I'd be the one enjoying you getting raped. Do you have any more rape stories like that one? Or even worse?

A knock on the door.

VIOLET: Well, let's find out.

She answers the door and lets LEO, in his late forties, tough and lean, into her apartment.

VIOLET: Leo. Hello. Nice of you to come. I was worried you wouldn't get my message.

LEO: What message? We talked on the phone.

VIOLET: Oh. That was actually your voice? Not a recording?

LEO: Jesus. Same old Vi.

VIOLET: Same as when?

LEO: Never mind.

VIOLET: I hope you like beef stew. I'm behind in my shopping, so it's out of a can. (*looking at him closely*) No... you look okay.

LEO: What?

VIOLET: I mean compared to how you could look.

LEO: And how is that?

VIOLET: Dead. You could look dead.

LEO: Yeah, well you tried your best.

VIOLET: Yes, I did. And I might have been wrong to do that.

LEO: You were definitely wrong. I had nothing to do with what Keith was up to.

VIOLET: There was evidence to the contrary.

LEO: No, there wasn't. It was all in your fucked-up mind.

VIOLET: Well, they must have believed some of what I told them, or you wouldn't have wound up in prison.

LEO: That was for an unrelated matter. And it only came to light because you tried to implicate me in those murders Keith committed.

VIOLET: Oh yeah. Something about... what? Something about... Help me out here, will you?

LEO: Extortion. I was extorting people.

VIOLET: Right. But not killing them?

LEO: No.

VIOLET: Or so it appeared.

LEO: Well none of them were dead, so it "appeared" pretty clear, didn't it?

VIOLET: Let's eat. Do you like beef stew?

LEO: You already asked me that.

VIOLET: And what did you answer?

LEO: I didn't.

VIOLET: So what's the big deal about me asking you again? Jesus, you're touchy. Is it from all that sodomization?

LEO: Look, you said you wanted to talk about something important.

VIOLET: Right. Then I invited you to lunch.

LEO: I came for the talk. Not to eat.

VIOLET: You have to eat before we talk. Especially after I went to all this trouble.

LEO: The trouble of opening a can?

VIOLET: The trouble of finding out what pisshole motel you were staying in, and then getting myself into a mental state whereby I could invite you into my home in order to get a few things settled without getting myself so upset that I can't be responsible for my actions.

LEO: That sounds like a threat. They tell me you're under a lot of restrictions, that you've been declared mentally incompetent or something, that you've been going through a lot of treatment.

VIOLET: Yes. It's been quite an adventure.

VIOLET is dishing out the stew from a pot.

VIOLET: Bread?

LEO: ... Sure.

VIOLET pushes the loaf of bread on the table towards him.

VIOLET: Help yourself to the butter. I remember you were always big on butter. Butter is probably a luxury in prison, right?

LEO: Yeah, it is.

VIOLET: Okay. So slather it on then.

LEO does. Takes a bite.

VIOLET: Good, eh?

LEO: (*eating*) Yeah.

VIOLET: Dip it. Dip it in the stew. I remember you liked doing that. You liked dipping things into other things. Keith thought it exposed your lower-class roots, but you didn't seem to care.

LEO: I didn't.

VIOLET: Yeah, that was the one time you ignored him and stood up for yourself. Too bad it was about something as silly as dipping bread. But whatever, you were finally going to be who you were, low-class warts and all. And the hell with anyone who had a problem with that.

LEO: Like you.

VIOLET: I never cared what you came from Leo. I just hated what you'd become.

LEO: You mean a crook?

VIOLET: And a vicious killer. Don't forget that part.

LEO: Of for Chrissake Violet. How long are you ... going ... to ... to ...

VIOLET: Something wrong?

LEO: I feel ... a little ...

He passes out and falls off his chair.

VIOLET: Yeah. Too much butter will do that to you. Well, that kind of butter anyway.

She begins to drag him by his ankles towards the bedroom.

VIOLET: Hope I didn't put too much of that stuff in. It wouldn't kill you, but it would make you very stupid. Too stupid to talk any sense. And we can't have both of us being like that, can we? How would we ever come to a reckoning?

Blackout.

SCENE 5

CATHY and VIOLET are on the couch. VIOLET
flips through a magazine. CATHY is reading
from a binder.

CATHY: (*reading*) "There are several kinds of anxiety disorders. People with these disorders respond to certain situations with fear and dread."

VIOLET: (*off a photo*) You'd look good in this. At least for a year or two. After that it could just make you look desperate for attention.

CATHY: "The fear and dread can manifest in a rapid heartbeat or periods of extreme sweating."

VIOLET: I don't have that.

CATHY: No, you probably don't. Then there are mood disorders, which "involve persistent feelings of sadness fluctuating with periods of extreme and/or manic happiness."

VIOLET: (*cheerily*) I *could* have that.

CATHY: Yes. You could.

VIOLET: But then again, so could you.

CATHY: Yeah, I know.

VIOLET: You do?

CATHY: Well, on my bad days I think I might be a little... But then I just tell myself, so fucking what, and I carry on. (*smiling*) But then there are psychotic disorders. And they involve "distorted awareness and thinking. That is, hallucinations and delusions."

VIOLET: You think that's the one, don't you?

CATHY: You killed your husband because you believed he was a serial murderer. You tried to kill your brother-in-law because you thought he was his accomplice.

VIOLET: So the hallucinations were ...?

CATHY: Seeing your husband shoot an elderly couple in that bakery ...

VIOLET: Which I did.

CATHY: Which you hallucinated. Keith was not anywhere near the bakery when that happened.

VIOLET: If you say so.

CATHY: You heard evidence in court that corroborated that.

VIOLET: If you say so.

CATHY: I say so because it's the truth.

VIOLET: If you say so.

CATHY: Violet. Listen to me –

VIOLET: In a minute. First tell me something. That couple was shot by someone, right?

CATHY: Yes.

VIOLET: And I saw that?

CATHY: Yes. You were there. In the back of the store when a masked man came in, robbed them, shot them, and ran out to a waiting car.

VIOLET: So that's not a hallucination.

CATHY: No, it's not. But Keith doing the killing and Leo waiting in the getaway car: that's a delusion.

VIOLET: So a delusion can be caused by something that's not a hallucination.

CATHY: Yes. No. Maybe. Knock it off, okay. You know that's not what I'm –

VIOLET: Here's what I think. I think it's delusional *not* to think it was Keith. I think the people who say they saw Keith in the tavern where he usually sat, just saw someone who looked like Keith. I think you should consider my theory.

CATHY: Violet. We're trying to maintain a connection to reality here. If we can't do that we have to re-evaluate the efficacy of both your medication and your therapy.

VIOLET: Truth is, it was just someone who looked like Keith sitting where Keith always sat. I think you should consider my theory.

CATHY: Why?

VIOLET: Why not?

CATHY: Because several doctors, a judge, and a prosecutor have all said repeatedly that your "theory" is just a response to your mental illness. You had a psychotic break. You wanted an excuse to kill your abusive husband, and you manufactured it. Come on, Vi. Can't you try to just admit that possibility for me? I could tell the doctors you did at least that, and then maybe we could pull back on your medication.

VIOLET: That's some incentive. Or is it a bribe?

CATHY: It's probably both. Does it matter? We need to show them that you're making progress.

VIOLET: Even when you think I'm not?

CATHY: I believe the restrictions on you should be ... relaxed. I think you need to get yourself back into the world to some degree. So if you'd just give over to admitting that it ... probably wasn't your husband who killed that couple ...

VIOLET: Sorry. Not that I don't appreciate the offer. But I'm seriously invested in holding on to my version.

CATHY: What's that mean?

VIOLET: It means I still believe in telling the truth. Even when people think I'm just a paranoid psycho.

CATHY: (*checking her watch*) I have to go. (*standing*) I'll be back tomorrow.

VIOLET: What time?

CATHY: I'm not sure.

VIOLET: Just roughly. Morning. Afternoon. When the sun sets?

CATHY: Probably afternoon.

VIOLET: Early or late afternoon?

CATHY: Probably late.

VIOLET: Three or four?

CATHY: Closer to four.

VIOLET: Okay. So let's say three forty-five probably.

CATHY: Approximately.

VIOLET: And probably.

CATHY: Okay. Yes. Probably.

VIOLET: Good. (*standing*) Are you okay?

CATHY: I'm fine. Are *you*?

VIOLET: Couldn't be better. (*off her look*) Just kidding. Of course I can be better. I know that. And I'm working hard on doing that. Not hard enough. But don't lose faith.

CATHY: I won't.

> CATHY *leaves.* VIOLET *rushes into the bedroom and almost immediately returns pushing a gagged and tied* LEO *on a chair with wheels.*

VIOLET: I bet you thought she'd never leave.

She removes his gag.

LEO: I have to take a piss.

VIOLET: Well, I'm not going to untie you. Do you want me to insert a catheter?

LEO: No, I don't want you to insert a fucking catheter.

VIOLET: Good. I'd have to make one from scratch, and who knows how well that would turn out? I guess you'll just have to wet yourself.

LEO: Untie me. Let me go.

VIOLET: Why would I do that?

LEO: Because there's no point in keeping me here like this, for God's sake.

VIOLET: Of course there is. I've got a world of people who won't believe me about what you and your brother were up to. So I need you to tell them the truth.

LEO: Which is what I've done for the last three years. Every time you've had another "piece of evidence" or you think you've remembered something I did or said, I've had to tell some cop the truth, so they could check it out. I've been questioned, checked out, and checked out some more. I'm innocent of the things you say I've done.

VIOLET: Oh you are, are you?

LEO: Yes, I fucking am! And you're nuts!! You were nuts when they threw you outta that school you worked at, you were nuts when you tricked Keith into marrying you, and you were nuts when you fucking killed him.

VIOLET: Okay, first off, I did not trick him into marrying me. He lied about that just to get a cheap laugh from his idiot pals.

LEO: (*a quick thought*) Yeah. That might be true. I'll give you that.

VIOLET: The truth is he tricked *me* by pretending to be a normal human being!

LEO: Okay, but some of the things I said about you are true, too. You could have turned Keith into the cops, instead of murdering him, for Chrissake.

VIOLET: I tried. They just ignored me!

LEO: Because you were a nutcase! And you still are. Look what you've done to me, Violet. You spiked the fucking butter so you could get me tied to this chair. Why would a sane person do something like that?!

VIOLET: Because I need to hear the truth.

LEO: About what?

VIOLET: About you! It's not like I don't have reasons to doubt myself, you know. I have strange thoughts and all kinds of impulses that make me do or say or think things. So I have a lot to overcome to hold on to my version of events. (*patting his head*) Please, Leo. I'm just asking for a little help here. Can you find it in yourself to help a poor soul like me?

    LEO starts to cry.

VIOLET: Why are you crying?

LEO: I think it's stress. I'm pretty stressed right now.

    VIOLET wipes away one of his tears.

VIOLET: Well, crying won't help. It never helped me, and I've cried a lot.

    Blackout.

SCENE 6

VIOLET is curled up on the couch. LEO is asleep in the chair. Still tied up. And gagged again.

A key in the door. MADDY comes in. She sees them and stops. She looks closely at LEO.

MADDY: Ah, Jesus... (*shaking VIOLET*) Mum... Mum!

VIOLET stirs, opens her eyes.

VIOLET: Oh hi, honey.

MADDY: (*checking out LEO*) What have you done to him?

VIOLET: Are you scared, darling? If you're scared you can just leave.

MADDY: No. I can't just leave. I tried leaving a while ago, and that didn't work out. It just made me sadder and more confused than I already was.

VIOLET: I have no idea what you're talking about, dear.

MADDY: Yeah, well, maybe that doesn't really matter anymore.

VIOLET: You could be right. I still love you, though.

MADDY: That's good.

VIOLET: Do you still love me?

MADDY: Absolutely. And there's nothing I can do about it. (*looking at LEO*) He looks drugged. Did you give him something?

VIOLET: A bit of something, yes...

MADDY: And... what were you hoping to accomplish by doing that?

VIOLET: Well, I needed his full attention. Or do you mean: why have I done it in this particular way? Well, things get out of control for me sometimes. I have an idea, then I have an idea how to realize that idea. But then before you know it, something happens that doesn't necessarily relate to what I intended to do in the first place. But this isn't like that. This is basically what I intended. So I think I might be getting better.

MADDY: I think we should try to wake him up.

VIOLET: Be my guest.

MADDY: (*shaking him*) Leo... Uncle Leo!

MADDY takes the gag out of his mouth.

MADDY: This smells like butter.

VIOLET: Yes. He loves the stuff. It was an act of kindness on my part.

LEO: (*waking up*) It's... got... something in it... that knocks you out. And keeps you that way. Hi, Maddy. I told you she was capable of some really scary shit.

VIOLET: Told her? Told her when?

LEO: When she visited me inside.

VIOLET: (*to MADDY*) You went to see him while he was in prison?

MADDY: He's my uncle.

VIOLET: So what? Most criminals have relatives of some kind. Doesn't mean they should feel obliged to visit them in prison. Did you take him things? Cookies and candy and whatever? You did, didn't you?

MADDY: Jujubes.

VIOLET: His favourite. I knew it! Don't get me wrong, I'm glad you're big-hearted, but show some judgment, for God's sake!

LEO: I don't feel so good.

MADDY: What was it you gave him, Mum?

VIOLET: It's a very strong sedative. They gave it to me when they thought I was just hysterical. I took a few. Then put the rest aside.

MADDY: Because?

VIOLET: Because I knew they'd come in handy one day. (*off LEO*) And here we are.

MADDY: Jesus… (*pointing at something on the couch*) What's that?

VIOLET: My meat cleaver. Just in case he got loose.

LEO: (*still trying to focus*) That's bull. She threatened to cut off my nuts with it.

VIOLET: (*to MADDY*) The way he talks. "Cut off my nuts." How did I get mixed up with that family? I've got three degrees, for God's sake.

LEO: So what? I was a stationary engineer.

VIOLET: (*to MADDY*) Means he was a janitor.

LEO: I took care of the boiler.

VIOLET: Janitor. You were a school janitor. (*to MADDY*) Which would have been fine if he was a good one. Good ones can make a difference in a school in terms of safety and cleanliness. He wasn't a good one.

LEO: Screw you. You know what you are. I mean, besides a lunatic. You're a snob! (*to MADDY*) Okay, kiddo. Untie me.

VIOLET: (*to MADDY*) No. Don't do that. He knows I'm on to him, and he'll try to silence us.

LEO: (*to MADDY*) Okay. We can sit here forever and listen to the crap coming out of her mouth, or you can untie me and we can all go about our business.

VIOLET: Which for him means killing us both.

LEO: Maddy. Just untie me, okay. Whatever she gave me is making me wanna puke.

VIOLET: Go ahead. "Puke." Who cares. (*off the stain on his pants*) He already wet himself.

MADDY: (*looking*) Ah, man ...

LEO: She wouldn't let me go to the toilet.

VIOLET: I offered to push the chair up close and aim his penis for him, but he didn't like that idea. (*to* LEO) Go ahead. Vomit. Mess yourself. You're not going anywhere until you confess to your crimes.

MADDY: Mum. We can't keep him here against his will.

VIOLET: You might change your mind when I show you the evidence.

> *VIOLET heads for the bedroom.*

LEO: What evidence? There is no goddamn evidence! (*to* MADDY) Look. Untie me. And I'll forget this ever happened.

VIOLET: (*offstage*) Don't do it, honey!

LEO: Maddy! Please. I'm getting kinda stressed out here. I had my heart checked out in prison, and the results weren't that good.

MADDY: Let's just see what she has. If we humour her for a while it'll be easier for all of us.

> *VIOLET returns with a large box, turns it over, and lets the contents spill out onto the floor.*

LEO: What the fuck's all that?

VIOLET: Your mother's diaries. I forgot I had them, and then one day there they were under my bed. She kept her eyes on you and your brother until the day she died. And when she knew that day was close at hand she gave them to me

for safekeeping. I figure it was to provide whatever proof
I needed against you.

LEO: She kept diaries? You actually want me to believe that
woman kept diaries?

VIOLET: (*off the box*) Well there's the proof. Right in that box.

LEO: Yeah? And what language are they in?

VIOLET: What's it matter?

LEO: Because she couldn't write more than ten words in English.

VIOLET: I had them translated.

MADDY: Who by?

VIOLET: I have friends who speak many different languages.

LEO: Right. And all of them are in your goddamn head. I'm
asking who you know in the real world who speaks what's-it-
called…

MADDY: She was Lithuanian.

LEO: Yeah, right.

VIOLET: Lithuanian. French. Greek. What's it matter. The
woman maybe couldn't write in English, but she spoke it well
enough to let me know what she thought of you and that she
highly suspected what you and Keith were up to. (*to MADDY*)
Assassins. Killers. They were hired killers. They worked for
anyone who could pay their fee.

MADDY: And Nanna knew this?

VIOLET: (*pointing*) It's all in there.

LEO: Bullshit. She had nothing to do with us. We saw her maybe
twice a year, Maddy.

VIOLET: She was a very intuitive woman. Plus there were
rumours. They both had a well-known tendency to violence.
People in the neighbourhood were afraid of them.

LEO: And that meant we were killers for hire? (*to* MADDY) Look, Maddy. Get this into your head, okay? You have to let me go, or you're in even more trouble than she is. I mean, you're not a certified loon, so you can be held responsible.

VIOLET: I've heard enough of him for now. Just the sound of his voice makes me want to harm him.

> VIOLET *is wheeling him towards the bedroom.*

LEO: I mean it, Maddy. You'll be in deep shit.

> VIOLET *rolls him in and closes the door. We can hear* LEO *protest incoherently through the door.*

VIOLET: (*returning*) Okay. We better get started. We're going to need a Lithuanian–English dictionary. Can you go get one?

MADDY: You mean they haven't actually been translated for you?

VIOLET: Well, how the hell would I arrange that confined to a psych ward? I just suspect what they say very strongly.

MADDY: Look, Mum ... I'm trying not to upset you. I've even tried to believe what you're saying. But Leo's right. I could get in a lot of trouble if I let you keep him prisoner here.

VIOLET: Okay. I hear all that. I've processed it. And I understand the core issue. But Leo's the solution to a lot of things that have gone wrong for me. Yes, I had some problems from when I was dealing with all those kids in my school who were determined not to reach their full potential. That was deeply depressing, and it made me feel like a failure. But your father and your uncle, what they were up to, sent me to a whole new level on the mental-health chart ... And the fact that I wasn't taken seriously about that ... well, it made cracks in my brain.

MADDY: Cracks.

VIOLET: Yeah.

MADDY: In your brain.

VIOLET: Yeah. Do you want me to tell you what that felt like?

MADDY: No, Mum. I never want to hear what that felt like. (*crying*) Promise that you'll never tell me, okay?

VIOLET: What's wrong, honey?

MADDY: Just promise.

VIOLET: Okay. Sure. That's a deal. Now go get me that dictionary. Bring it back here. And give me a fighting chance to get the truth out of that guy in there. Then you can just leave.

MADDY: Leave. But with Leo still tied up.

VIOLET: It's a compromise solution.

MADDY: No, it's not. He'll tell people I let you keep him captive.

VIOLET: No one will believe anything he says. Look, I think I have proof in black and white that he's a lying thug who, at the very least, was your father's assistant in fifteen or so murders.

MADDY: Mum.

VIOLET: Please, honey. The dictionary. It's crucial to my investigation.

MADDY: Yeah ... okay. But promise you won't hurt him.

VIOLET: Promises, promises. Of course I won't hurt him. He has to answer to a jury of his peers!!

MADDY: Okay. Good. Where do I get that? The dictionary.

VIOLET: Bookstore. Library. Maybe online. Maybe google it. Use your basic intelligence. You're not an idiot, are you?!

MADDY: Calm down, Mum. I was just –

VIOLET: Okay, right. I mean, even if you are a bit of an idiot, you're my daughter and I should show you nothing but love.

MADDY: Well, as long as it's not too much effort.

VIOLET: It's just that sometimes when I look at you or I hear you ask questions like that, you remind me of your father. And I have to suppress an urge to hurt you a little. You understand that, don't you?

MADDY: Sure. He used to say that to me, too.

VIOLET: That he wanted to hurt you?

MADDY: That he thought I might be too much like you. He'd catch me daydreaming, and he'd snap his fingers in front of my face. "Careful girl. Whatever's going on in your head right now, you should stop. When your mother gets that blank look on her face it's because she's barely hanging on to sanity."

VIOLET: He said that?

MADDY: All the time. *He* said you were out of your mind. *You* said *he* was a murderer. Yeah. Those were fun times all right. And now this! Uncle Leo's a prisoner. And I'm actually helping you keep him that way. All because you've told me things I don't completely understand. Unless I do. Unless I do actually understand everything you say in some deeply disturbed way because I'm totally like you. Yeah. I must be. (*starting out*) Oh my God...

VIOLET: No, it's okay.

MADDY: Is it? Because it doesn't feel okay. Not really.

MADDY leaves.

VIOLET: (*shouting down the hall*) Don't worry, dear. It could be just a phase.

Blackout.

SCENE 7

MADDY is on the floor searching through a
printout of a Lithuanian–English dictionary.
VIOLET is on the couch behind her, massaging
MADDY's shoulders.

VIOLET: Both my parents had died that year and I was
desperately searching for a little joy in my life. Just the
kind of person a sociopath targets. The first sign that I was
in trouble was when he started voicing his views about
immigrants. He was brutal and unforgiving about all their
trouble with the language. I tried to point out that his
parents were in exactly the same shape when they came
over. "I know," was his reply, "and that's why I hated being
around them." His father was very ill at this time, and
neither of his sons wanted anything to do with him. I'd
help his mother when I could, but being the wife of an evil
sonofabitch can have an effect on you. Then you came along
and that helped for a while. No way was I going to become
completely mentally incapacitated when I had a child to care
for. Anyway ...

MADDY: There's a title for this diary, *The Troubling Story of
Henrikus and Leonas.* Leonas is Uncle Leo, right?

VIOLET: Yes. And Henrikus was your father.

MADDY: He changed it to Keith?

VIOLET: No, he just started asking people to call him that at
some point.

MADDY: Did he give any reason?

VIOLET: He never explained any of the strange things he did.
Like putting pepper on grapefruit, or drawing pictures of rats.

MADDY: What?

VIOLET: I have nothing to add about that. (*pointing*) Try to translate that opening paragraph.

MADDY: Okay. But it'll take some time.

VIOLET: It's important. I might have to use it as evidence. If I can put Leo in prison for the rest of his life, I'm hopeful that my mental state will improve.

MADDY: You seem better today. You took your medication?

VIOLET: Only half. It helps me achieve a degree of clarity. But it makes me lose touch with my true self.

MADDY: Okay. But what is that, Mum? Your true self. I mean, really.

VIOLET: Hard to describe. But it includes a vibrant inner life.

MADDY kisses VIOLET's hand which rests on her shoulder.

MADDY: I love you.

VIOLET: Do you? Still?

MADDY: Yes. I love you. Even when you're not sharing your vibrant inner life with me.

VIOLET: What a nice thing to say.

VIOLET kisses the top of MADDY's head. A loud groaning is heard coming from the bedroom.

MADDY: I guess he woke up.

VIOLET: Yeah.

VIOLET takes the butter from the kitchen table. She puts her hand in it, takes a fistful, and heads for the bedroom.

VIOLET: This should keep him quiet for a while.

MADDY: Mum...

VIOLET: What, dear?

MADDY: (*looking at her*) Never mind.

VIOLET continues into the bedroom.

MADDY: We'll just deal with it somehow.

Blackout.

SCENE 8

*As CATHY comes into the apartment, MADDY
hurries to put the diaries back in the box.*

CATHY: Family stuff?

MADDY: Yeah.

CATHY: Letters? Photos?

MADDY: Some. Yeah.

CATHY: Could I have a look?

MADDY: Now?

CATHY: Why not now?

MADDY: Well, now is just ... now. What about ... a future now?
I mean, that now could be better, right?

CATHY: Sure, whatever. Anyway it's good that you're getting her
to reconnect to things.

MADDY: Well, here's hoping.

CATHY: And it's great that you're seeing her more.

MADDY: Yeah.

CATHY: She missed you.

MADDY: I know. But it couldn't be helped. I needed some time
on my own. In the desert.

CATHY: Which desert?

MADDY: (*an outburst*) Why is that any of your fucking
business?! Sorry! There it was again.

    CATHY looks at her.

CATHY: How long were you in therapy?

MADDY: No, I was never in –

CATHY: Oh. It's just that I was in court when the judge strongly suggested that you talk to someone.

MADDY: Yeah. Well, my husband was still listening to me at the time. And he has quite a few creepy men in his family.

CATHY: None like your father though?

MADDY: No. My father was a special kind of guy.

CATHY: So you still think your mum was right about him?

MADDY: I always try hard to lean in that direction, yeah.

CATHY: Even in light of her condition?

MADDY: It's been a struggle. And sometimes I need to challenge her about it. But well... her condition was caused by her knowing what he did, right?

CATHY: Not according to people at the school where she worked. They thought she was on the verge of a –

MADDY: That was just stress. She thought she was letting her students down. Look, the truth is, what I saw of my father's behaviour means I don't have that big a problem believing he was a cold-hearted killer.

CATHY: You'd seen him hurt people?

MADDY: Yeah.

CATHY: Did he hurt you?

MADDY: I got pinned to a wall a couple of times. I was never his main target though.

CATHY: Are you saying that was Violet?

MADDY: If he had ever hit my mother, I'd have killed him myself. It was Leo he liked to abuse. Ever since they were kids.

CATHY: And you heard that from your mother?

MADDY: It was a well-known fact in the neighbourhood. No one ever tried to stop it because they loved ugly, cruel shit like that around there. Not all of them, but there were a lot of mean people. Older men for sure. I think they were upset about missing the party.

CATHY: What party?

MADDY: You know, all the butchering they could have done back in their homelands. Eastern European countries were full of Nazis. Per capita, almost as many Germany. At least that's what my dad said. And he said it with a lot of pride too.

A noise from the bedroom.

CATHY: Should we look in on her?

MADDY: No, she's okay. Those pills just knock her out.

CATHY: She'll get used to them. If she keeps taking them every day they'll help her function.

MADDY: Well, I'll try to make sure she does. But she can be pretty stubborn.

CATHY: And sneaky. You know, we can manage this. I'm sure it doesn't seem that way now, but –

MADDY: I believe you. I just think it would help if you started believing *her* about my father and his brother.

VIOLET comes out of the bedroom, carrying the dish of butter.

VIOLET: I'll second that opinion.

CATHY: Hi there.

MADDY: Had a good nap?

VIOLET: I dreamed of a somewhat better world.

CATHY: Really. What was it like?

117

VIOLET: The air was a little cleaner. But not all the bad people were gone.

CATHY: What's the butter for?

VIOLET: I ... put it on my ...

MADDY: Her ... eyelids ...

VIOLET: Yes, on my eyelids before –

MADDY: She –

VIOLET and MADDY: Goes to sleep.

VIOLET: I find it relaxing.

CATHY: (*a bit suspicious*) Really? I'll have to try that.

VIOLET: (*about to hand her the butter*) You can take this.

MADDY: (*intervening*) Come on, Mum. I'm sure she's got her own butter at home.

VIOLET: Not like this.

CATHY: I'm sorry?

MADDY: (*taking the butter*) She means it's ... Danish. The best butter there is. Right, Mum?

VIOLET: Sure. (*to CATHY*) She has very strong opinions about food products.

CATHY: Well she *is* a chef.

MADDY: Was a chef.

CATHY: Oh. What are you now?

MADDY: An unemployed chef.

CATHY: So what happened?

MADDY: I got tired of being yelled at. The head chef was one of those bad people the world hasn't gotten rid of yet.

VIOLET: You didn't stab him, did you? You know our agreement about that. Just count to ten.

MADDY: (*big smile*) It doesn't always work.

CATHY: Does that mean you *did* stab him?

MADDY: No. I was just –

A commotion in the bedroom.

VIOLET: Excuse me. Something must have fallen off a shelf.

She takes the butter from MADDY *and goes into the bedroom, closing the door behind her.*

CATHY: Why did she take the butter in there with her?

MADDY: Habit?

LEO screams from the bedroom.

CATHY: Was that her?

MADDY: Who else could it be?

CATHY: Good question.

CATHY heads for the bedroom door.

MADDY: Cathy...

But she is already on her way in. MADDY *just lowers her head.*

MADDY: Jesus...

Blackout.

SCENE 9

LEO is on the couch, still a bit groggy. CATHY is wiping his face with a damp cloth. MADDY is bringing LEO a glass of water from the kitchen. VIOLET is standing near LEO, watching him intently.

VIOLET: (*to LEO*) Ready to talk?

LEO: Go to hell.

VIOLET: Just checking.

CATHY: What made you think you'd get away with this?

VIOLET: I'm crazy. I can get away with almost anything.

CATHY: That's actually not true.

LEO: Right. Who are you, anyway? You sound like someone official.

CATHY: I am.

LEO: Good. Well here's a couple of questions for you, then. How come she's not still put away somewhere? How come she's allowed to be on the loose like this?

VIOLET: (*to CATHY*) Yeah, I thought they were taking quite a risk myself.

MADDY: Me too. Sorry, Mum. (*to CATHY*) She just needed to find out.

CATHY: Find out what exactly? If she was still capable of doing something this reckless?

VIOLET: You make it sound so petty. (*to MADDY*) You'll have to be more specific.

MADDY: She needed to know for sure if he wasn't actually involved in those murders.

CATHY: And?

VIOLET: And what?

CATHY: And... *is he?* Did he admit to that?!

VIOLET: Well, he's a pretty stubborn guy. At first I wanted to waterboard him. But the farther we got into the diary the more pity I felt for him.

CATHY: What diary?

MADDY: His mother kept a record of their lives. His and my father's.

VIOLET: It's ugly stuff.

MADDY: Yeah, we've been reading it.

LEO: Whaddya mean, reading it? I told you, she couldn't write English.

MADDY: We translated it.

VIOLET: The original is in his native tongue.

LEO: I don't have a fucking native tongue.

VIOLET: You *did*. Your fucking native tongue was Lithuanian. You spoke it for the first three years of your life. It's in the diary.

LEO: In the diary?! In Lithuanian?!! And you fucking translated it?!!

VIOLET: Jeez. Calm down, man. You're going to have a stroke.

MADDY: We're still at it. We downloaded a dictionary. And it's slow going, but –

VIOLET: But we already know a lot about how your brother treated you.

LEO: You mean that he was a little rough on me sometimes? That was just brother stuff.

MADDY: According to Nanna he put you in the hospital twice. They thought for a while that Grampa was responsible.

LEO: That sad little man? Jesus. If I'd heard anyone talking crap like that ... (*crying*) I loved my pop. And he loved me.

VIOLET: Then why didn't he protect you from Keith? And didn't I advise you about crying? It's not going to help.

LEO: (*trying to stop crying*) Okay ... but it's upsetting ... All these ... lies ... and things you're telling me.

VIOLET: It's all in the diary, Leo. Keith beat you up repeatedly. And you were terrified of him.

LEO: Just when we were kids, for Chrissake. That all stopped when we grew up.

VIOLET: We don't think that's true.

MADDY: We think Keith never stopped pushing you around.

VIOLET: You're a victim of domestic violence, Leo.

LEO: What? Fuck off.

MADDY: You were traumatized and defenceless, Uncle Leo.

VIOLET: And that's why you kept doing everything he told you to do. Even when he told you to help him kill all those people.

LEO: That's not fucking true!

VIOLET: Yes, it fucking is!

CATHY: Okay, okay! Let's just all –

LEO: (*to CATHY*) I want you to inform the authorities about what she's done to me here. (*crying*) Talk about being traumatized and defenceless ...

CATHY: I can't do that.

LEO: (*still crying*) Why not?!.

CATHY: Because my job is to assist in her journey back to good mental health. And that wouldn't help.

VIOLET: She means I'm on to something.

LEO: Fuck it. (*standing*) I'll do it myself then.

MADDY: That'd probably be a mistake. She's got proof now.

LEO: Proof of what? Jesus. Come on.

VIOLET: Sit down.

LEO: Look, don't tell me what to do, okay? I'm tired of you asking me questions. I'm tired of you assuming things. And I'm tired of you telling me what the fuck to do. Like to just piss my pants ... or suck on butter. Or –

CATHY: Suck on butter?

MADDY: We can leave the butter out of it, okay?

VIOLET: Leo.

LEO: What?

VIOLET: Sit down. I mean it. We need to resolve this matter right here. Right now. I've got all these things happening in my head. All these thoughts, memories, suspicions. And lots of voices telling me what to think about all those things. I need it all to go away. I need to silence the voices of suspicion.

    LEO sits.

LEO: (*to CATHY*) She's been talking like that to me for two whole days ... that "voices of suspicion" crap. It makes me want to rip my ears off. Can you please, *please* make her stop?

CATHY: No. But maybe you can.

MADDY: Just tell her she was right about what my dad did. All those killings.

VIOLET: The old couple in the bakery. That woman lawyer. The entire family down the street. Their son was one of my students. Did you know that?

LEO: (*quietly*) No...

MADDY: What?

LEO: No. I didn't... know that. (*to* VIOLET) I'm sorry...

VIOLET: Killing that boy was the thing that set me off. (*to* CATHY) I blew Keith away a week after that happened.

CATHY: You knew he'd done it?

VIOLET: I asked him.

CATHY: And he admitted it?

VIOLET: No. But he didn't deny it.

LEO: I'm sorry.

VIOLET: Yeah, you said that.

LEO: That was supposed to be just the father. He owed someone a lot of money. But the family, that boy... I never drove Keith after that. I mean, I wouldn't have... even if you hadn't killed him.

MADDY: And that's all you did for him, drive?

LEO: Yeah. And it was bullshit. He didn't need a getaway car. He was really good at it. He could usually just walk away quietly afterwards and no one woulda been the wiser.

CATHY: Sounds like he just wanted you to be involved.

LEO: Maybe. Keep me on a leash? That kind of thing?

CATHY: Yes. That kind of thing.

LEO: Okay. Okay then. So... that's that, right?

> LEO *starts out, then stops.*

LEO: (*to* VIOLET) I feel better telling you. It's been a real hardship to keep it to myself. By the way, I won't do so good in prison. I didn't do that good the first time, and this would be worse.

VIOLET: I know.

LEO: I never did any killing. Honest.

VIOLET: I know.

LEO: Good. Okay then. (*looking at them all*) So ... if it's okay with everyone, I'll just ...

LEO leaves.

CATHY: Pathetic.

MADDY: You mean him? Yeah ... How does this affect her situation?

CATHY: You mean with the law? I haven't got a clue. And as far as her mental state is concerned ...

MADDY: We'll just have to see if this helps?

CATHY: You mean the bit of clarity he provided her? Yes.

CATHY looks at VIOLET.

CATHY: Maddy, we need to talk about her medication and a few other things.

VIOLET: Not in front of me, you don't. I've heard enough about my "treatment" and my situation to last a lifetime.

CATHY: (*to* MADDY) In the bedroom then?

MADDY: Sure.

CATHY and MADDY head for the bedroom.

VIOLET: Thank you.

CATHY: You're welcome.

VIOLET *is just sitting there.*

VIOLET: (*to herself*) Silence. How about that. (*touching her temple*) Even in here... (*smiling*) it's been awhile.

Blackout.

SCENE 10

Darkness. The building's fire alarm goes off.

Light.

VIOLET *is on the couch, rocking back and forth, and covering her ears.*

VIOLET: Okay. Okay. Just turn it off... come on, turn it off, for Chrissake! (*rocking*) You rotten little bastards! It's mean. And it has to stop! Someone has to make it stop! (*grabbing the cleaver and rushing out*) Okay then, maybe this will do the trick!

Blackout.

SCENE 11

VIOLET is helping LEO into the apartment. He has been roughed up: a bloody nose and a welt under his eye.

VIOLET: You were very brave out there.

LEO: Well, I couldn't let them keep screaming at you like that.

VIOLET: (*helping him sit*) Yeah, I guess threatening to castrate them got them pretty worked up. I mean, after I explained what that was.

LEO: They should be way more understanding of your condition.

VIOLET: Please don't refer to my condition as a "condition."

LEO: I just meant... well, even when you were accusing me of all that stuff with Keith, I cut you a certain amount of slack.

VIOLET: That was big of you. Considering that everything I said was true.

LEO: Except you told people I was a killer.

VIOLET: I had a reason for that.

LEO: Yeah, you were out of your head.

VIOLET: No. It was something else. (*thinking*) Yeah. It was Keith. When no one knew who was doing those killings, Keith told me he thought it could be you.

LEO: Why would he do that?

VIOLET: Let me think about that for a moment. What were you doing hanging around in front of the building?

LEO: I never left.

VIOLET: ... Because he was planning to kill you.

LEO: What?

VIOLET: That's why he told me you might be the killer. He was planting suspicions about you in people's heads. (*thinking*) Yes. And then once he'd done that, he'd plant evidence that *pointed* to you. Then he'd kill you, and make it look like self-defence. At least that's what *I'd* do. What do you mean you never left?

LEO: Well, I didn't know where to go. I mean, should I head back to the motel, should I go into hiding, should I go drown myself in the fucking lake? I mean, when I saw Maddy and whatshername head off, I was sure they were on their way to turn me in to the cops. And I can't go back to prison! I just can't!!

VIOLET: Okay, okay, try to relax. Maddy had to pick up the kids from school. And *Cathy* was probably going shopping. Trust me, she hasn't got anything on her mind except what to do with *me*.

LEO: And what about you?

VIOLET: The last time I reported someone to the police I wound up in a psych ward.

CATHY comes in, carrying a bag of groceries.

CATHY: What's he doing here?

VIOLET: He saved my life.

LEO: And I got a little banged up in the process.

CATHY: You're talking about the incident in front of the building?

VIOLET: Yes, I am. What have you got there? More lousy canned goods?

CATHY: You told me, very emphatically, that you only wanted to eat food from a can.

VIOLET: That was because of the spiders. (*to LEO*) I was afraid there were spiders hiding in all the fresh vegetables.

CATHY: Right.

VIOLET: Right. But you convinced me that there weren't.

CATHY: I did? You know, you have to tell me when that happens, Violet. When I tell you something that's actually real or true, you have to let me know that it's sunk in, okay?

VIOLET: Sure. No need to make a big deal about it, though.

CATHY: Got it. So fresh fruit and vegetables are okay, then.

VIOLET: Like I just said, yeah.

CATHY: (*to LEO*) The police are looking for you.

LEO: (*to VIOLET*) You said she wasn't gonna report me.

VIOLET: I guess I was wrong.

LEO: Looking for me. Jesus... I mean, they might think I'm armed.

CATHY: I didn't tell them you were armed. I just told them you were an accomplice in a number of murders.

VIOLET: That sounds worse than it is.

CATHY: I think it sounds just about right, actually.

LEO: Okay, but the thing is, it could mean they'll be ready to shoot me on sight.

VIOLET: (*to CATHY*) He's right. He'll need to be accompanied to the police station. (*to LEO*) She'll do it.

CATHY: No, I won't.

VIOLET: Why not? You're the one who put him in jeopardy.

CATHY: I'm not taking this guy to the police station. If I have to take anyone there, it'll be you. They want to talk to you, too.

VIOLET: About what?

CATHY: About threatening all those kids with that freakin' cleaver. You promised me that was only for chopping meat.

VIOLET: And did you ever bring me any meat? No. So there it was, just lying around without a purpose. Maybe if you tell the cops I was just very nervous...

CATHY: I did. I tried to explain your entire situation. But they still want to see you.

VIOLET: Promise you won't let them put me in prison.

CATHY: That's not going to happen.

VIOLET: What about a hospital? Can you promise to keep me out of a hospital too?

CATHY: I'll do my best.

VIOLET: Okay. I'm okay with that.

LEO: You can take us both.

VIOLET: I was just about to suggest that.

VIOLET starts for the door.

CATHY: (*to herself*) Great. A little family outing.

LEO: I'm pretty stressed about what's going to happen. You'll need to shield me, so they don't gun me down.

VIOLET: Thinking ahead to possible consequences, eh? I guess that's a habit you picked up in prison? (*to* CATHY) Leo was a target for sexual predators.

VIOLET leaves.

LEO: (*to* CATHY) It wasn't anything I couldn't handle.

CATHY: If you say so.

CATHY leaves.

LEO: (*to himself*) I do. I do say so.

LEO leaves, closing the door behind him.

Blackout.

SCENE 12

MADDY is waiting for VIOLET to come out of the bedroom.

MADDY: How you doing in there, Mum?

VIOLET: (*inside the bedroom*) I'm fine, sweetie.

MADDY: You don't have to fuss, you know.

VIOLET: Of course I do. I want to look just right for the kids. You sure they're on the way?

MADDY: Yeah. Definitely. Cathy's bringing them. But she wanted a chance to talk to them first.

VIOLET: About what?

MADDY: Well, you know ... just about how (*to herself*) fucking weird things might get.

VIOLET: What was that?

MADDY: Well they haven't seen you for a while and you've been under a lot of pressure, so –

VIOLET: I don't like the sound of that. Suppose she exaggerates my health issues. She's inclined to do that, you know. And it might make the children pretty nervous ...

MADDY: Yeah ... (*to herself, a bit too loud*) That's the issue alright!

VIOLET: What?

MADDY: No, no, don't worry. She's a professional. She knows how to handle these things.

VIOLET: If you say so.

MADDY: The basic thing ... The only really important thing is that the kids are really looking forward to seeing you. So ... just try to stay calm and –

VIOLET: Don't worry. It's going to be terrific fun! (*coming out of the bedroom*) Ta-dah!!

> *She is dressed in a clown outfit. The total package: nose, hair, cheeks, big shoes.*

VIOLET: I've been saving all this for years. Wanted them both to be old enough to enjoy it. Whaddya think?

> *MADDY is just staring at her.*

VIOLET: Honey? I need to know what you think about my outfit.

MADDY: Do you? Really? Okay then... (*a deep breath*) I think... it's great!

VIOLET: You do?

MADDY: Oh yeah... it's –

VIOLET: Perfect? Is it perfect?

MADDY: Perfect? Sure! It's totally perfect! (*to herself*) Too fucking perfect...

VIOLET: Good. Whaddya think Cathy will make of it?

MADDY: She'll probably be a little concerned.

VIOLET: Yeah. Dosage. We'll need to have a long talk about my dosage.

MADDY: Probably. Yeah. And mine too.

VIOLET: But the kids will love it, right? And that's all that matters.

> *She honks her nose. CATHY knocks and enters. Sees VIOLET. Stops. Stares.*

MADDY: It's just something special she's doing for her grandchildren.

CATHY: No. No. It's not...

MADDY: You think it's too much?

CATHY: No. Well it could have been too much, but it doesn't matter because –

MADDY: Where are the kids?

CATHY: Down in my car with their father.

VIOLET: Why didn't you bring them up?

CATHY: Well they ... changed their minds.

VIOLET: Because of something you said?

CATHY: No, it was –

MADDY: (*to CATHY*) What happened?

CATHY: Someone took a video of your mother menacing those kids with her ... cleaver. It was on the news.

VIOLET: Really? Such a small thing to be featured on the news? I mean, with the world about to explode and all?

CATHY: One of Dennis's friends texted him the video while I was trying to explain things to the children.

MADDY: And he showed it to them? Idiot!

MADDY takes out her cell and punches speed dial.

CATHY: It's gone viral, by the way.

MADDY: Great ... (*on the phone*) Hey. What the hell were you thinking? (*heading into the bedroom*) Well, maybe we could have talked about it first! ... Whaddya mean, why?! Jesus Christ! Don't go anywhere. I'm on my way down!

MADDY disconnects and starts out.

VIOLET: Don't hurt him, okay?! People sometimes make mistakes?

MADDY: Yeah. Big ones.

CAHTY: Count to ten! Okay? Just count ...

But MADDY *is gone.*

CATHY: (*to herself*) ... to ten.

VIOLET: (*to* CATHY) You were a little slow getting that out.

CATHY: Yeah...

VIOLET: I guess I won't be seeing them anytime soon.

CATHY: There are consequences for our behaviour. Even when we're not entirely responsible for that behaviour.

VIOLET: Was that one of those things you say that I need to acknowledge?

CATHY: Yes.

VIOLET: Okay. I understand what you're saying.

CATHY: And what it means?

VIOLET: I suppose it means I have to be more heavily medicated.

CATHY: Not more heavily. Just more consistently. And it also means you're going to be monitored more closely.

VIOLET: In a hospital?

CATHY: Unless you'll agree to letting a health worker move in here.

VIOLET: You?

CATHY: No.

VIOLET: Well, that's good. The proximity might damage our friendship.

CATHY: We have people who do that short term.

VIOLET: Well, that's quite a choice, isn't it? Give up my privacy by being in a hospital. Or give it up in the comfort of my own home.

MADDY *comes back in.*

CATHY: That was fast.

MADDY: Coward took off before I got down there.

VIOLET: With my grandchildren?

MADDY: Yeah. Look, I can fix it with the kids, but it'll take some time.

CATHY: (*to* VIOLET) You hear that? It's going to be okay eventually. Just try to be patient. (*starting out*) And you've got a court appearance tomorrow morning. I'll pick you up at 9:30.

VIOLET: Are they going to put me in jail?

MADDY: (*to* CATHY) What's she talking about?

CATHY: (*stopping*) I told you I wouldn't let that happen.

MADDY: Neither would I.

VIOLET: A hospital would be bad enough, but jail...

> *They both look at* VIOLET. CATHY *sits beside her on the couch.*

CATHY: I'll always try to do what's best for you. I care about you very much, Violet. Please try to believe that. We all do. All the doctors who work on your case. All the people who love you.

VIOLET: Who are they?

MADDY: You mean besides me?

CATHY: And me. I love you too.

> VIOLET *takes off her nose and puts it on* CATHY.

VIOLET: Say that again.

CATHY: I love you. And I admire you. And so do those other teachers you worked with. They admire you as well. Not to mention all those young people you taught.

VIOLET: Especially the ones I couldn't help. I'm sure they have great respect for my capability.

MADDY: Mum…

VIOLET: It's okay. (*to CATHY*) You can take off that nose now. It's starting to make me nervous.

CATHY: (*taking it off*) Why a clown anyway? Why not a pirate or a … vampire?

VIOLET: I wanted to make them laugh. Clowns make kids laugh. Don't know why. They're obviously the work of the devil.

CATHY: I agree.

VIOLET: You do? Gee. I was only kidding about that. You might need some help yourself when you finish with me.

CATHY: I don't think I'm ever going to finish with you, Vi. I think we're stuck with each other for a long time.

VIOLET: You probably didn't mean that in a bad way. So try to rephrase it, okay?

MADDY sits on the other side of VIOLET.

MADDY: (*to CATHY*) Yeah, say something like … Well, here we are in a difficult, real-life situation, all of us with a need to stay connected. Both personally and professionally.

VIOLET: (*continuing*) All in our own ways struggling for answers. All in our own ways trying to make the best of very complex circumstances…

CATHY: And we keep trying. We don't give up.

VIOLET: Even when it seems foolish, and even painful, not to.

MADDY: (*putting on the nose*) We don't ever give up, Mum. Okay?

VIOLET: I'll do my best.

MADDY puts her head on VIOLET's shoulder. VIOLET puts her hand on CATHY's head, and gently pushes it down onto her other shoulder.

Blackout.

THE END

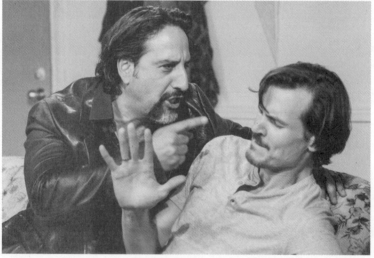

TOP: Ron Lea (Harry) and Anne van Leeuwen (Lacey) in *Kill the Poor* at the Assembly Theatre in Toronto, Ontario (October 27 to November 18, 2018).

BOTTOM: Al Bernstein (Mr. David) and Craig Henderson (Jake) in *Kill the Poor*.

KILL THE POOR

PRODUCTION HISTORY

Kill the Poor was first produced by Leroy Street Theatre at the Assembly Theatre in Toronto, Ontario, Canada, from October 27 to November 18, 2018. It played as a double bill with *Her Inside Life*, produced by Low Rise Productions. The cast and crew were as follows:

LACEY	Anne van Leeuwen
JAKE	Craig Henderson
HARRY	Ron Lea
ANNIE	Chandra Galasso
MR. DAVID	Al Bernstein

Director	Wes Berger
Assistant Directors	Breanna Dillon and Marisa McIntyre
Stage Manager	Jenna Borsato
Set Designer	Chris Bretecher
Lighting Designer	Chin Palipane
Sound Designers	Jeremy Hutton and Will Jarvis
Costume Designer	Kathleen Black
Graphic Designer	Fook Communications

SETTING

An apartment in a one-bedroom low-income five-storey building.

CHARACTERS

LACEY, late twenties
JAKE, late twenties
HARRY, mid-fifties
ANNIE, mid-to-late thirties
MR. DAVID, late forties

SCENE 1

> *An apartment in a low-rent five-storey building.*
> *Open to a kitchen and a small eating area. A door*
> *to the bedroom. In the living room, a couch, a TV*
> *on a stand, and a single weathered armchair.*
> *The apartment is messy. Clothes on the chair*
> *and couch.*
>
> *Some mumbling. A thud against the door.*
> *A WOMAN groans in pain from out in the hallway.*

LACEY: Careful.

JAKE: Okay...

LACEY: (*groaning*) I said be careful!

JAKE: Okay!

LACEY: Jesus. Just ... pay attention.

JAKE: I am!

> *The door opens and JAKE and LACEY, both in their*
> *late twenties, enter. JAKE is helping LACEY into the*
> *room. She looks tired and unsteady.*

JAKE: Into the bedroom?

LACEY: No, I'm okay on the couch for now.

JAKE: Yeah, but I made up the bed.

LACEY: I don't wanna get into bed. I've been in a bed for
two weeks.

JAKE: Right. So the couch then.

LACEY: Like I said.

> *JAKE leads LACEY to the couch and tries to*
> *lower her.*

LACEY: Take it easy...

JAKE: Yeah.

LACEY: (*looking around*) There was no time to tidy up a little, eh?

JAKE: Yeah. No. Sorry.

> *JAKE is picking up clothes from the couch, tossing them, and lowering LACEY at the same time.*

LACEY: I said easy! God!

> *LACEY is down.*

JAKE: You okay?

LACEY: I wanna stretch out.

JAKE: Yeah, good idea.

> *JAKE lifts LACEY's legs onto the couch. She stretches out.*

LACEY: Can you get me a glass of water?

JAKE: Sure... (*heading into the kitchen*) Anything else?

LACEY: No.

JAKE: Your lunch was still on the tray beside your bed.

LACEY: So what?

JAKE: (*returning with water*) So you should eat. Just because you didn't like the food in the hospital, doesn't mean you –

LACEY: I'm okay.

JAKE: I could make you some scrambled eggs.

LACEY: No. Just sit down.

> *LACEY drinks the entire glass of water.*

LACEY: We need to talk about Tim's funeral.

JAKE: Really? You wanna talk about that now?

LACEY: I know it's something you don't wanna deal with. But I'm not up to it, and there's no one else.

JAKE: What about your mother?

LACEY: Really? She just lost her son, Jake. She can barely bring herself to talk. You gotta step up here, okay?

JAKE: Yeah. Sure. But I've never arranged a funeral.

LACEY: Call someone. Wayne's wife died last year. You could ask him what you need to do.

JAKE: Wayne from the laundromat? I can't ask him shit like that!

LACEY: Sure you can. Just get him to give you a list.

JAKE: A list of what?

LACEY: Of things we need to do, for Chrissake. (*holding up her glass*) Here.

JAKE: Another one?

LACEY: Yeah...

> *JAKE takes it, heads into the kitchen.*

LACEY: Actually, this time, put it in a measuring cup. I'm supposed to be keeping track of my fluid intake.

JACK: Why?

LACEY: So they can tell if the kidneys are getting back to full... kidney stuff.

> *JAKE returns with an empty measuring cup.*

LACEY: (*off the empty measuring cup*) There's no water in that.

JAKE: Right. Sorry.

> *JAKE heads back to the kitchen.*

LACEY: It's hot in here. What's the thermostat at?

JAKE: Doesn't matter. It's broken.

LACEY: Really broken? Or just kinda wonky like usual.

JAKE: No, it's fucked.

JAKE's back with the water.

LACEY: Jesus. Did you call Harry?

JAKE: Who?

LACEY: (*taking the glass*) The maintenance guy.

LACEY drinks.

JAKE: His name's Harry? I thought it was Sonny. I've been calling him Sonny for two years. Guy must think I'm an idiot.

JAKE starts out.

LACEY: Whoa, where are you going?

JAKE: I need to apologize to him.

LACEY: Right now?

JAKE: (*stopping*) No. Not right now. But soon. Because calling the guy the wrong name for two years is just fucking rude, and I think he deserves an apology!

LACEY: Hey. What the hell's wrong with you? You're way too worked up!

JAKE: I know that! You don't think I know that?

LACEY: So, why?

JAKE: Whaddya mean why? You could've died! I mean, Jesus Christ, Lace!

LACEY: Yeah. Okay. But –

JAKE: I mean, I could be here by myself right now! And what would I do then? Do you think I want to live without you?

LACEY: You'd be okay.

JAKE: No, I fucking wouldn't.

LACEY: Well, not right away.

JAKE: Not ever. Jesus. You die. I die too. Right away. I mean, as soon as I can figure out how to do it.

LACEY: Okay, let's not –

JAKE: I mean it. Do you believe me?

LACEY: I don't know. Maybe. But it doesn't matter. Because I didn't die! And I am here. Okay?

JAKE: Yeah.

LACEY: So, maybe you should just go with that for now.

JAKE: Okay, yeah. I'll try to accept that.

LACEY: Good. So did you call him?

JAKE: Who?

LACEY: Harry. The maintenance guy? (*off his look*) About the thermostat?

JAKE: Right. Yeah. He came and looked at it.

LACEY: And?

JAKE: He thinks it's fucked, like I told you.

LACEY: Okay. And is he planning to fix it?

JAKE: He said he'll get someone. He doesn't know how to do it himself.

LACEY: He doesn't?

JAKE: No. He hasn't got a clue.

LACEY: Really? So what's the point of having a maintenance guy if he can't fix things?!

JAKE: He's pretty good at cleaning. The floor in the lobby is always really shiny –

LACEY: Shiny. Jesus. Look, just tell him we need that thermostat fixed. Winter's coming, man. It's a health issue.

JAKE: Okay. I'll talk to him. (*starting off, then stopping*) But not right now, right?

LACEY: Right. But when you do, find out if he's ever had to bury someone.

LACEY's cellphone goes off. She takes it out and looks at its screen.

LACEY: It's that cop. (*offering her phone to JAKE*) You talk to her.

JAKE: She's calling you.

LACEY: Just take it.

JAKE: No...

They just watch the phone until it goes silent.

JAKE: You gonna call her back?

LACEY: No.

JAKE: Well, you're gonna have to talk to her sometime.

LACEY: Fuck her. She's just looking for someone to blame.

JAKE: Well, someone is to blame.

LACEY: Maybe. Or maybe it was just an accid– Look, the point is, do you think she's hassling the other guy like this?

JAKE: You can ask her that when you call her.

LACEY: Didn't you hear me? I'm not doing that. When do you have to be at work?

JAKE: Marco gave me the day off. I told him I had to pick you up and –

LACEY: With pay? (*off his look*) Are you getting paid for this time off, Jake?

JAKE: I'm not sure.

LACEY: Okay. So then you better get going.

JAKE: And leave you alone? No. It's just a day's pay, so what's it matter, really?

LACEY: Well, if you look through all those bills on the dresser you'll see why it matters. I bet a lot more have come in during the last couple of weeks too.

JAKE: Yeah...

LACEY: So, go ahead then. Walk into the bedroom. Open them up and take a good look at them.

JAKE: I can't.

LACEY: Come on. I know it's not much fun but –

JAKE: I threw them out. (*off her look*) Well, it was too much. Just watching them pile up. And you were in the hospital, and your brother was in that coma... and it was all just too much.

LACEY: So, you just threw them out.

JAKE: Yeah.

LACEY: And did that make you feel better?

JAKE: Kinda. It was like a fuck you to all of them. Like I didn't have enough shit on my mind. Was I just supposed to just forget about the accident, sit down, write them all their cheques, and then send them off with a note apologizing for being late like you do sometimes?

LACEY: That bothers you, does it? You like it better when they're calling us all the time?

JAKE: Look, all I'm saying is that throwing them out felt a lot better than paying them would have.

LACEY: Well, good for you. But our credit cards are probably being cancelled.

JAKE: Big deal. We'll use cash.

LACEY: As long as we have it. We live off those credit cards between your paycheques. When my EI gets spent there's always a few days when...

JAKE: When what?

LACEY: We need to eat.

JAKE: Yeah, okay, the credit cards are important. I'll call them and say we lost the bills.

LACEY: Sure. That'll work. No, just tell them about the accident. That should buy us some time. Our phones are probably overdue too. And was there anything in that pile from the landlord?

JAKE: Like what?

LACEY: Like an eviction notice.

JAKE: Why would we be getting evicted? We pay the rent. Don't we?

LACEY: Yeah...

JAKE: On time?

LACEY: On time... most of the time. But people are saying they might be selling the place.

JAKE: Yeah. But that's just a rumour, so –

LACEY: Go to work. Please, just go to work.

JAKE: Sure. I'll make you something to eat and then –

LACEY: No. I'll be fine. Just go!

JAKE: Okay... yeah...

He kisses her.

151

JAKE: You know, maybe I can ask Marco about funerals. He's got a really big family, and some of them have probably died, right?

LACEY: Right. But I don't see Marco being the guy they'd trust to make the arrangements.

JAKE: Yeah, I know you think he's not that smart but –

LACEY: I think he's a fucking idiot. Is he still watching porn on his phone while he fixes those cars?

JAKE: It's a hard habit to break.

LACEY: What is? Watching porn? Or doing it when you're putting in a new oil filter? Never mind. Just get going. He's probably already docking your pay.

JAKE: Yeah … (*starting out*) I love you. You know that, right?

LACEY: Yeah, I do.

JAKE: And I'm so fucking glad you're … you know …

LACEY: Alive?

JAKE: Right.

> *He kisses her again, then leaves.* LACEY *sighs, lies down, inhales deeply, but feels a sudden pain.*

LACEY: Ah, shit. (*yelling*) Jake!? … Jake!!

> *She struggles to get up.*

LACEY: (*weakly*) Come back …

> *She collapses on the floor.*

> *Blackout.*

SCENE 2

A little later. Building manager HARRY, *in his mid-fifties, is helping* LACEY *back onto the couch. His tool chest is on the floor.*

HARRY: Were you attacked?

LACEY: (*a little out of it*) No... I just...

HARRY: Fainted?

LACEY: What?

HARRY: Fainted!

LACEY: Yeah...

HARRY: I ask because the door was unlocked, and there are some people in this building who might take advantage of that. I'm not saying who. But it's better to be careful. And an unlocked door is –

LACEY: What are you doing here?

HARRY: Oh. Well, I was feeling bad about all the things I never had fixed for you. So I thought I'd try to take care of that. I mean, I knocked and when there was no answer I reached for my master key but I'd forgotten it, then just to be sure I turned the knob, and... here I am. You don't look so good. Do you want me to call an ambulance?

LACEY: No.

HARRY: Then maybe I should call your husband at work.

LACEY: No, that's not a good idea.

HARRY: Are you sure? I mean, generally speaking, people like to be notified about things like this.

LACEY: Well, he's been "notified" a lot lately.

HARRY: Right. The accident. That musta been a kick in the head. So yeah, we should just leave him alone then.

LACEY: He can't leave work, anyway. His boss will dock his wages.

HARRY: Under these circumstances? No fucking way. Guy must be a real prick, eh?

LACEY: It's a small garage. And I think it's a struggle to keep it going. But yeah, he's definitely a prick.

HARRY: Yeah. And what's the point of keeping a business open if you're not going to behave decently to your employees? Better to just close up shop and shoot yourself in the head. Well, maybe that's an overstatement. But if more people believed that treating others decently is the most important thing in life ... then it'd be a better world, right?

LACEY: (*to herself*) A better world ... Who says things like that?

HARRY: I do? You look like you're in pain. Is that from falling down? Or do you look like that all the time? I mean, since your accident. That was one brutal collision, wasn't it?

LACEY: So they tell me. I don't remember.

HARRY: Really? Well that's not good. You had a brain scan?

LACEY: Yeah, but –

HARRY: Brain injuries can fuck you up for life. And that accident ... it was in the papers, pictures and everything. It looked really bad. I figured nobody could have survived that. Not if they were in that small car, anyway. But that was yours, wasn't it? So –

LACEY: Yeah. Look, can you do me a favour? Fill that measuring cup with water.

HARRY: Sure.

He takes it and goes into the kitchen.

HARRY: (*from the kitchen*) Someone was killed though, right?

LACEY: My brother. He was in a coma for a few days, but then he –

HARRY: (*returning*) Your brother. Ah Jesus, that's rough.

He hands her the cup of water. She downs it.

LACEY: (*off his look*) I'm measuring my intake because my kidney was damaged.

HARRY: Your kidney? Maybe your brain. That's pretty serious shit. And what about that other guy? He was hardly hurt at all, probably. He was driving a beast, right? What was that, an Escalade or something? And your car was –

LACEY: A fifteen-year-old shit box.

HARRY: Yeah. So no contest. I mean, here comes your little shit box. Here comes the Escalade. And SMASH!! What a fucking nightmare that musta been! (*wincing*) Sorry. That was too ... I mean, it pisses me off, but I should try to keep it under control. What's it to you how I feel about it? Are you going after the guy?

LACEY: Whaddya mean?

HARRY: Well, he's probably got money, right? That thing he was driving costs a fortune.

LACEY: He says we ran the light.

HARRY: That true?

LACEY: Maybe. I don't know.

HARRY: Any witnesses?

LACEY: None so far. It was pretty late.

HARRY: So, it's just his word on the subject?

LACEY: The cops believe him, I think.

HARRY: Yeah? Well here's hoping that's not because he's got some PR company protecting his ass. Just be ready to deal with that bullshit, okay? I mean, if it starts to feel like you're getting screwed. Look, I better get to work because these things take me awhile to fix for some reason. Might be a hand-eye coordination problem. Toilet first.

HARRY heads down the hallway with his tools, but suddenly returns.

HARRY: One more thing. You need to find a witness. And you need to do it before he finds one. If you know what I mean. Do you? Do you know what I mean?

LACEY: No. I don't.

HARRY: Well I haven't got time to explain it now. I've got a toilet to fix.

He leaves again. LACEY picks up her phone and punches a key.

LACEY: (*on the phone*) Hi, Jen. How's she doing? ... Has she been out of bed? ... Well, try to get her up, or she'll just lie there thinking about it all day. Maybe get one of her other friends to come over. No. I'm out now ... Yeah, I'm a lucky girl.

A knock on the door.

LACEY: No, it's okay. I know what you meant.

Another knock.

HARRY: (*off*) Someone's knocking.

LACEY: (*covering her phone*) I know. (*on the phone*) Look Jen, I gotta go ... Yeah, I will. Bye.

Another knock.

HARRY: (*partially in the room*) Do you want me to get that?

LACEY: Please.

HARRY: Do you know who it is?

LACEY: No ...

HARRY: Do you want me to get it anyway? I mean, suppose it's that guy.

LACEY: What guy?

HARRY: From down the hall. You know, the guy?

LACEY: You mean the dealer. Why would it be him?

HARRY: He does stuff like that.

LACEY: Knock on doors?

HARRY: Usually just when he's high. The thing is, he doesn't just sell. He's a big user. I guess he never heard of the "Ten Crack Commandments." (*off her look*) You know, from Biggie Smalls ... Commandment four: "Never get high on your own supply."

A much louder knock.

LACEY: Look, are you gonna get that or what?

HARRY: Sure ...

He heads off. The sound of a door opening. A few muffled words.

HARRY returns. Detective ANNIE Regan, mid- to late thirties, is standing by the door.

HARRY: (*to LACEY*) She's a cop. Says she wants to talk. You okay with me letting her in?

LACEY: Yeah, it's fine.

HARRY: Good. And is it okay if I keep working? Because I'm not sure when I can get back to it.

ANNIE: (*fully entering*) Busy guy, are you?

HARRY: Yeah, I am ... (*starting off, then stopping*) Excuse me. Was that meant to be sarcastic? Because if it was, it would have been unnecessarily rude.

ANNIE: You're right. It would have been. But it wasn't.

He looks at her hard, then leaves. ANNIE *watches him go, then turns to* LACEY.

LACEY: Hi.

ANNIE: Yeah, hi.

LACEY: Look, I was going to call you back. I wasn't up to talking before, but I was going to –

ANNIE: Sure. But I was close by anyway. So ...

LACEY: So, it's important then. I mean, talking to me couldn't wait?

ANNIE: Well, waiting is what I've been doing, Lacey. The accident took place fifteen days ago. And there are questions to ask.

LACEY: Sure. But ...

ANNIE: You still can't remember anything?

LACEY: Not really. I remember a sound now. The sound of it came back to me.

ANNIE: The sound of the collision?

LACEY: Yeah. Like a big explosion or something. And someone screaming. I think it coulda been me.

ANNIE: So just those sounds? And nothing more?

LACEY: Well, I remember being in the ambulance.

ANNIE: Okay. But nothing before that? How about when you were in that field?

LACEY: What field?

ANNIE: Beside the intersection. That's where you and your brother were found. I told you that.

LACEY: You told me I was found in a field? Sorry. I don't –

ANNIE: Yeah, that's where you were, alright. So that's a mystery. I mean, your car was totalled, and it sure didn't look like anyone who was injured like you and your brother were could have made it out of that car and into that field. Not without help anyway.

LACEY: What about the other driver? Maybe he –

ANNIE: He was still in his vehicle ... unconscious when EMS got there. He remembers the accident happening. But then he passed out.

LACEY: How's he doing?

ANNIE: He's got a slight concussion. Some bruising.

LACEY: Really? So it wasn't such a big deal for him?

ANNIE: I didn't say that.

LACEY: You kinda did. And he's still saying the accident wasn't his fault?

ANNIE: He's saying your car ran the light, yeah. He doesn't know if it was you or your brother driving. But he's sure his light was green.

LACEY: Well, maybe I should start saying our light was green.

ANNIE: Except you've already told us you don't remember.

LACEY: So maybe I do now.

ANNIE: Do you?

LACEY: (*looking at her first*) No. I fucking don't. But maybe he doesn't either. Or maybe he's lying, for Chrissake. Have you thought of that?

ANNIE: It's crossed my mind. Look, the investigation at the scene was inconclusive, so –

LACEY: So why not leave it at that? Call it an accident? Why are you looking for someone to blame?

ANNIE: Because when your brother Tim died it meant that this became a possible case of vehicular homicide. Unless he was the one driving...

LACEY: And then it's... what? Vehicular suicide? Jesus Christ!

ANNIE: Well, we can't charge dead people with a crime, can we? So...

LACEY: So that just leaves me...

ANNIE: Look, I think you need to rest for a few more days. Why don't you do that? Rest. Get better. I'll be back. Okay?

LACEY: Whatever.

> *ANNIE leaves. HARRY comes back in carrying a plumber's wrench.*

HARRY: I heard all that. Yeah, you're definitely going to need a witness.

> *Blackout.*

SCENE 3

JAKE is setting the table for dinner. We can hear LACEY from the bathroom.

JAKE: In the field.

LACEY: That's what she said.

JAKE: With Tim...

LACEY: Yeah. Both of us. Like I told you.

JAKE: I just can't get my head around it.

LACEY: (*appearing*) So until you can, are you gonna keep asking me questions about it?

JAKE: (*going into the kitchen*) Am I bugging you?

LACEY: A little.

JAKE: (*returning with a large pot*) Maybe you're just hungry.

LACEY: (*sitting*) What's that?

JAKE: Pasta. It's a recipe Marco told me how to make.

LACEY: What's in it?

JAKE: (*serving*) Tomato sauce. Olives. Onions... Sausage. Plus there's something I forgot... Maybe sugar. Anyway it looks good, right?

LACEY: No, it looks gross.

JAKE: Try it. If you don't like it, just say so.

LACEY: (*trying it*) I don't like it.

JAKE: Really? He said everyone likes it. Do you want me to add sugar, just in case?

LACEY: No, that's okay. All those ingredients. How much did they cost?

JAKE: Well the sausage was kind of – Why?

LACEY: You could have just made potato soup or something to save money.

JAKE: Can we just for one night not talk about money?

LACEY: Okay. For one night. But not this night. How are we gonna pay for Tim's funeral? Five grand. I mean, that's a lot.

JAKE: Marco says it's probably the cheapest we can get away with. It'll just be a plain coffin. And there won't be any extras.

LACEY: What are the "extras"?

JAKE: I don't know. But we can't have them, whatever they are.

LACEY: Well, as long as they don't include things like people to dig the hole.

JAKE: That's pretty dark, Lacey. You're worried it'll be just us digging a hole for him to go into?

LACEY: It's probably my pain killers. I'm gonna go off them.

JAKE: Good plan... Listen, are you totally sure Tim didn't have life insurance?

LACEY: He hadn't even had a job for five years.

JAKE: Okay, but he sold dope. Maybe he had some cash put away?

LACEY: He sold a little weed. He wasn't like the guy down the hall.

JAKE: You mean Daryl? Yeah, he's impressive.

LACEY: Impressive?

JAKE: I mean successful.

LACEY: Maybe he's just lucky. I mean, he's not following the Commandments, right?

JAKE: The Commandments? Like, from the Bible?

LACEY: No. From Biggie Smalls.

JAKE: Oh. Right. Yeah, because he does it from his apartment. "Never sell crack at a place you'll be at." That's number five, I think. Or are you talking about number four? "Never get high –"

LACEY: "– on your own supply." Yeah. So he does both ...

JAKE: Definitely. He's a risk taker. So you know about them? The Commandments?

LACEY: Just that one. It sounds like you know them all.

JAKE: Well, they're legendary.

LACEY: You mean for people who sell crack.

JAKE: Yeah. Or did. Even if it was only part-time.

LACEY: Part-time as in "not 24-7"?

JAKE: Yeah. I was never 24-7. (*off her bowl*) Maybe eat just a little? To get your strength back?

LACEY: Sure ... (*taking a mouthful*) No. Sorry. Maybe some apple sauce. Or canned peaches.

JAKE: Okay.

He heads into the kitchen.

JAKE: I need to ask you about that field again.

LACEY: Jesus ...

JAKE: Is it possible in any way that you can think of, or even just imagine, that Tim got you out of that car and then –

LACEY: He had a broken back, Jake. They told me he was probably killed on impact.

JAKE: Okay. But ... maybe he didn't know that.

LACEY: What?

JAKE: Well, sometimes people are dead and it hasn't hit them yet. They just act on nerves or something.

LACEY: You mean like a chicken after its head's cut off? He wasn't a fucking chicken, Jake.

JAKE: I know that. But maybe he was acting like a chicken.

LACEY: Jesus Christ. What is wrong with you?

JAKE: I'm scared.

LACEY: Of what?

JAKE: That cop for one thing! It sounds like she's really into finding out how you wound up in that field. And I'm just trying to come up with something that will get her off your back.

LACEY: Try harder.

JAKE gets a text.

JAKE: It's from Harry. He's coming up.

LACEY: Yeah, he's got a plan.

JAKE: For what?

LACEY: I better let him tell you. I'm not sure I totally understand it.

A knock on the door.

LACEY: Is that him already?

JAKE: No. He said he'd be a while.

JAKE heads to the door. LACEY forces down another mouthful of the pasta dish. JAKE returns with MR. DAVID, a late-forty-ish man in a dark suit and turtleneck.

JAKE: This man wants to talk to us. He says it's –

LACEY: (*to MR. DAVID*) You're the guy...

JAKE: What guy?

LACEY: In the accident. In the SUV.

MR. DAVID: So you saw me then?

LACEY: No. I mean ... I guess so. What do you want?

MR. DAVID: Well a few things, actually. First, I'd like to know how you're doing.

LACEY: Okay. How are *you* doing?

MR. DAVID: A little dizzy still. But mostly pretty good. Lucky, I guess.

JAKE: It was more than luck, man. When that thing you were driving plowed into them it musta felt like they were getting hit by a tank.

MR. DAVID: (*to LACEY*) Did it?

LACEY: I don't remember.

MR. DAVID: Yes, I was told you were having a problem with that. And the memory hasn't improved?

JAKE: Why? You worried she might be able to contradict your story?

MR. DAVID: No. I'm hoping she can support it. It's not good having my version of what happened be the only one.

LACEY: Sorry. Can't help you.

JAKE: She can't even remember how they got in that field.

MR. DAVID: Excuse me?

JAKE: They were found in a field beside the intersection.

LACEY: Do you know anything about that?

MR. DAVID: I was unconscious. Maybe someone who was passing ...

165

LACEY: Maybe...

MR. DAVID: Anyway. I feel bad about your car. Bad that I was driving something that could cause that much damage.

JAKE: And kill her brother.

MR. DAVID: Yes. Well I can't do anything about that. I truly wish that I could. But about the car...

He takes out a cheque and puts it on the table.

MR. DAVID: That should put you in something... decent. (*off their looks*) No strings. Just wanted to help you in some way... That's it then. I'll let myself out.

He takes in the apartment, smiles a little, then leaves.

JAKE: Did you see that? The way he smiled when he was taking in our apartment.

But LACEY is looking at the cheque.

LACEY: Jesus...

She hands it to JAKE.

LACEY: We could buy two of our cars brand new for this.

JAKE: Maybe three.

A knock on the door. HARRY enters, carrying a binder.

HARRY: Your door was unlocked again. That's no good. If you do that often, try to stop. There are people in this building who never learned the basic rules of how a society should function.

JAKE: (*to LACEY*) He means they steal.

LACEY: (*to HARRY*) We've got nothing worth their time.

JAKE: She means we decided not to let it freak us out.

LACEY: People can get desperate. That's just the way things are.

HARRY: That's very compassionate. But also a little soft-headed. Did you think like that before your brain injury?

JAKE: (*to* LACEY) What's he talking about?

LACEY: Nothing. (*off* HARRY's *binder*) What's that?

HARRY: Our petition. We'll get to that later. But first we have to talk about the witness situation.

JAKE: You mean the fact that there isn't one?

HARRY: Not yet.

LACEY: That's his plan. To get a witness.

JAKE: You mean to find one?

LACEY: No, to get one. To make one up.

HARRY: Well, not from scratch. It'll have to be a real person capable of answering all the questions that'll be asked.

LACEY: Like?

HARRY: Well, why didn't he or she come forward earlier? It's gonna be tricky.

LACEY: And illegal.

HARRY: But also very satisfying. Because the other guy has to compensate you for all the damage and pain he caused.

JAKE: He says it wasn't his fault.

HARRY: The witness will say otherwise. I'm telling you, he has to pay.

LACEY: He already has.

She shows him the cheque.

HARRY: He sent this?

JAKE: No. He was just here.

HARRY: He was? How'd he find out where you live?

LACEY: Good question.

HARRY: (*off the cheque*) So, this is guilt money.

JAKE: Yeah, but not for the accident. For the size of his vehicle...

HARRY: He said that?

JAKE: Kinda...

HARRY: Okay, it's a start. But there's no way you can accept... (*off the cheque*)... fifty grand as compensation for the death of your beloved brother.

LACEY: But suppose it really wasn't his fault.

HARRY: That will become less and less important as we proceed. Also, from now on, don't talk to him without having your lawyer present.

JAKE: We don't have a lawyer.

HARRY: Yes, you do. You're looking at him.

JAKE: You're joking?

HARRY: No, I'm exaggerating. I have no technical right to call myself that since my disbarment. (*receiving nothing but stares back*) Okay, here it is in a nutshell. I was at a low point in my life, and my only client was a wealthy elderly woman. I was both her lawyer and her chauffeur, and when she died I handled her estate. She had intended to leave all her money to animal shelters in memory of the twenty-six Pomeranians that had so enriched her life, which I think was a fine idea, but not when your young lawyer is struggling to pay his rent or even eat properly.

LACEY: So you took some of it.

HARRY: Yes. And when it was discovered, they took away my right to practise my chosen profession. But not, and this is important, my ability to get things done. So, back to the witness issue... and where to find this person. It can't be anyone close to home.

JAKE: So, none of the criminals in this building.

HARRY: We don't want a criminal, period. We want someone who understands that people like you need to occasionally receive a little justice. Let me mull it over. It's important to get this right. Because there will be a lot of money involved.

LACEY: If the guy was heavily insured?

HARRY: Oh no. We're not going that route. He won't publicly admit to being responsible for killing your brother.

LACEY: Especially if he didn't do it.

HARRY: Again, let's not dwell on that. Besides, that won't be the issue if he thinks we have someone who says he did do it. Which he might have anyway. Correct?

JAKE: Yeah. Because we only have his word that he didn't.

HARRY: But wealthy people with influence walk away from this kind of thing all the time. Because the authorities, and fuck them all the way to hell for it, go out of their way to exonerate them. (*gagging*) Excuse me. This kind of injustice fills my mouth with vomit... Speaking of injustice, I want you to sign the petition.

> *He opens the binder.*

JAKE: What's it for?

HARRY: We're not getting evicted. No matter what the owners want to do with this place. We're all staying put. Oh there's going to be a struggle. But let's see them try to throw out three hundred people who are vigorously resisting that action. This isn't just a petition. It's a declaration of war. Now, are you both going to sign or what?

LACEY: I am. We're in no position to find another place to live. First and last month's rent. The cost of moving...

JAKE: What are you talking about? We've got that guy's cheque.

HARRY: No. Sorry. You have to return it. It could look like you've accepted a settlement. No wait, you should hold on to it in case our plans turn to shit. But don't cash it. Under no circumstances, until we've exhausted all other options, do you cash it. Okay?

They look at each other, turn back to him, and nod.

HARRY: Fantastic. Now back to the witness thing. First off though, any chance I can get a cup of tea?

JAKE: Coffee okay?

HARRY: If that's what you've got then that's what I'm having. Asking for things that people don't have is something that should definitely be discouraged. It only causes embarrassment. (*standing*) Mind if I use the bathroom?

LACEY: Go ahead.

HARRY leaves.

JAKE: He could be getting us involved in things we can't handle.

LACEY: Suppose we can, though. Suppose we can handle those things and even more. And suppose we wind up with a lot of money.

JAKE: That's a lot of supposing.

LACEY: Yeah. But maybe we should've started doing it a long time ago. Supposing things. Instead of just dreaming things.

HARRY returns.

HARRY: Got it! We need a communist. A good old-fashioned "let's redistribute the wealth" totally out-of-her-fucking-mind pinko!

He gives them an enthusiastic thumbs-up. They return it, quite a bit less sure.

Blackout.

SCENE 4

ANNIE is in the armchair looking at her notebook.
LACEY is making her way from the bathroom to
the couch.

ANNIE: How's the urine?

LACEY: Sorry?

ANNIE: Any blood?

LACEY: No...

ANNIE: Good. And the output?

LACEY: It seems to be okay.

ANNIE: So, it looks like you're going to be fine then. Now if we can just get that memory back, eh?

LACEY: Yeah, well, that'll either happen or it won't.

ANNIE: Makes you kind of vulnerable, though. I mean, something could come to light that points us in a certain direction that... leads us to a certain conclusion. And if you're not able to remember –

LACEY: Are you fucking with me, Detective?

ANNIE: Yeah. I am.

LACEY: Why?

ANNIE: I was hoping to shake you up, spark something in your memory bank. Look, I'll be honest with you. If there's any doubt in this case, the other driver, Mr. David, is almost certain to receive the benefit of that doubt.

LACEY: So I've been told. Why, though?

ANNIE: Well, in this case it might be because both you and your brother have criminal records.

LACEY: For things that have nothing to do with driving a car.

ANNIE: (*reading from her notebook*) No, but public intoxication, possession of a controlled substance, assault, two failures to appear for him and one for you ... they don't look good when we're trying to figure out who messed up at that intersection.

LACEY: Was I drug-tested in the hospital?

ANNIE: You, the driver of the other vehicle, your brother ...

LACEY: You tested my brother while he was in a coma?

ANNIE: Procedure. Everyone was clean. So, good on you. For getting yourself sober. But then there's your husband ...

LACEY: What about him?

ANNIE: He dealt drugs.

LACEY: Who told you that?

ANNIE: Other drug dealers.

LACEY: He has no record.

ANNIE: You mean he was never caught. Right. But it still makes it look like your family isn't exactly law-abiding. And again, if we're looking to find fault ... Now, that won't mean much if it's determined that your brother was driving.

LACEY: Because you can't jail a dead man. I got that the first time you mentioned it.

ANNIE: Did you? Good. But on the other hand, if it's proven that you were driving ...

LACEY: Right. Vehicular manslaughter. Got that, too.

ANNIE: So, what are the chances?

LACEY: That I was driving?

ANNIE: Well, the car was in your name.

LACEY: Yeah. But he's the one who used it most of the time. What's going on here? These visits, these questions that are all kinda the same. It's like you're trying to wear me down or something. I mean, I don't remember anything, so why keep asking?

ANNIE: Maybe I'm just exploring options for you. For example, it's possible that, with a little help, it could be determined that Tim was driving. If that turned out to be the case then no one would go to jail and no one would be held financially responsible. I'm assuming Tim had no assets?

LACEY: He had a new pair of Adidas. (*off her look*) No, I get it. You mean I wouldn't go to jail and there'd be no reason to come after me or my mother for money. Okay... so here's hoping it goes my way. I mean, so what that my brother is fucking dead? And so what if that prick in the SUV might be lying about who had the green light? Because that doesn't matter, does it?

ANNIE: It does to me. But it might not to anyone else. And that includes a judge or a jury.

LACEY: Really? So what should I do?

ANNIE: You should remember. You should remember that Tim was driving.

LACEY: (*looking at her*) You want me to lie.

ANNIE: I want you to remember.

LACEY: Remember that Tim was driving. Just that?

ANNIE: Nothing else matters, Lacey.

LACEY: I'm not going to blame my brother, my dead brother, for something I don't know he did. Fuck you!

ANNIE: Come on, don't be stupid! You want to take a chance on making your life even worse than it is? Look hard at your situation, for God's sake. Look at this place. You've got nothing! You hear me? Nothing!

LACEY: Okay. Shut the fuck up.

ANNIE: What's wrong with you people?

LACEY: "You people"?

ANNIE: Yeah, you fucking ridiculous people. I don't know how or why it turned out for you like this. No money, no options, no future to speak of.

LACEY: Holy fuck. Listen to yourself!

ANNIE: It's just a goddamn mess, isn't it? Maybe you were born into it. Maybe shit just happened. But it's time to get real, okay? And try to make this one sensible choice, for Chrissake!

LACEY: You gotta go.

ANNIE: Really? You think that's your best move here? Kicking me out when maybe I should be allowed to wait for your husband to get home. He might be able to understand what I'm offering here. Nothing I've observed about him leads me to believe that, but I live in hope.

LACEY: We don't do that.

ANNIE: Do what? Live in hope?

LACEY: We don't disagree about things like this.

ANNIE: Really? Where is he anyway? He can't still be at work at 10 p.m.

LACEY: What are you getting at?

ANNIE: Just ask him who he's been hanging with when he gets home.

LACEY: Sure...

ANNIE: No, I mean it. Because just maybe he's been out doing something you might not agree with.

174

ANNIE is on her way out.

LACEY: Like what?

ANNIE: Just ask him.

LACEY: Like what?!

ANNIE is gone.

LACEY: (*sitting*) Fuck!

Blackout.

SCENE 5

LACEY is in the chair. She is holding three zip-lock baggies, one containing a white powder, one some pink pills, and the third some small chunks of crack.

Sound of the door opening. She puts the baggies under her. JAKE comes in. She looks at him.

JAKE: Hey...

LACEY: Yeah. Hey.

JAKE: How you doing?

LACEY: Not so good.

JAKE: How come? The pain bad today?

LACEY: No, that's under control.

JAKE: So, what's the –

LACEY: The cops know. (*no response*) Did you hear me? The cops know what you're doing.

JAKE: I'm not doing anything.

LACEY: You're dealing again.

JAKE: No way!

LACEY: That detective was here.

JAKE: And she told you that?

LACEY: Pretty much, yeah.

JAKE: Well, she's wrong. I mean, they might have suspicions but –

LACEY: Why? Why would they have suspicions?

JAKE: Well, the cops could've seen me with Daryl, I guess.

LACEY: Daryl?

JAKE: (*gesturing*) Yeah. You know ... from down the hall.

LACEY: Oh, you're working for that genius?

JAKE: No.

LACEY: No? Then what's this?

She produces the baggies. No response.

LACEY: Don't. Don't ... Don't fry your brain trying to come up with an excuse. We're way past that. That's us ten years ago. All I want to hear from you now is the fucking truth.

JAKE: Okay. Okay ... but I'm just doing it until ...

LACEY: I told you I don't want to hear any excuses.

JAKE: Well, what about a reason? A reason isn't an excuse, it's a ... fucking reason. And mine is that we need to get money for Tim's funeral.

LACEY: Not by doing this. What is all this shit anyway? That's crack but –

JAKE: And that's meth. And the other one is Apache powder –

LACEY: What?

JAKE: Fentanyl.

LACEY: Jesus. No fucking way. Fentanyl? That kills people.

JAKE: I don't fucking care.

LACEY: What?!

JAKE: I don't mean I don't fucking care. I just ... Okay, I'll give that one back to him.

LACEY: You'll give them all back to him.

JAKE: No. We need to get your brother out of the morgue and into the ground. That funeral home wants a deposit of fifteen hundred to even get started. And you made me not cash that cheque!

LACEY: Our lawyer said we shouldn't.

JAKE: You mean Harry? He was dis–, dis– ...

LACEY: –barred! Disbarred!

JAKE: Right. So he's not really a lawyer then, is he?

LACEY: Sure he is. Just like you're really a drug dealer. I mean, neither of you have forgotten how to do it, so –

JAKE: Please don't get yourself upset.

LACEY: Right. You wouldn't want that. You love me too much to see me upset, don't you?

JAKE: I love you more than anything. You're my whole life.

LACEY: Right. Okay. So why would you (*off the baggie*) leave this here so I could find it?

JAKE: Why would I want you to find it?

LACEY: Because you need to get me involved.

JAKE: Involved in what way?

LACEY: Could be a lot of different ways. Maybe you want me to talk you out of it.

JAKE: I don't.

LACEY: Well, maybe it's something else then. You do this shit all the time. You try to drag me into things for all kinds of reasons. You wanted me to take that mechanics course with you.

JAKE: I thought you'd like it.

LACEY: You thought I'd be good to have around in case there was any math involved.

JAKE: Come on.

LACEY: It took me five minutes. (*off his look*) To find this stuff.

JAKE: Really?

LACEY: Five minutes, tops.

JAKE: (*looking at her*) Well, I guess I forgot how good you are at it. You know, from all those years you spent trying to find where your mother hid her booze?

LACEY: And you're bringing my mother into this because…?

JAKE: Because I think she's why you're not always very trusting. I mean, you were searching for the drugs, right?

LACEY: Because that lady cop gave me a tip.

JAKE: Which you could have ignored. And I'm saying your mother's drinking is why you got sucked right into that problem we have with trust.

LACEY: You know, I thought we made a deal not to bring our parents into whatever goes wrong for us.

JAKE: Yeah, that's right. But you can't always ignore –

LACEY: My mum, your dad. We don't blame them, okay? We don't look back and find excuses. And we don't repeat. We don't do the stupid things they used to do just because they look easy.

JAKE: Unless we don't have a fucking choice.

LACEY: Oh. So we can make exceptions? You can sell meth and fentanyl, and I can get smashed and turn a few tricks?

She throws him the bag.

LACEY: Take it all back.

JAKE: That's not a good idea.

LACEY: I mean it. Take it the fuck back or I will.

JAKE: It won't matter who takes it back. The deal was made. "When you take it, you got it." That's a thing Daryl takes very seriously.

LACEY: The hell with what he takes seriously. That's some bullshit dealer code or something?

JAKE: No, it's all about business. He took what he gave me off the market, without cash up front, just on my say-so. And also he knows where I live so that was added security for him, right?

LACEY: Which means he can get to you.

JAKE: If he has to.

LACEY: And slit your throat.

JAKE: It won't be like that. I'm just responsible for his losses if I don't move it in a reasonable amount of time. He'll just add interest to what I owe him until I get it done. No big deal. Daryl says it's based on the rules of commerce. Sort of like a bank.

LACEY: What a load of crap. Interest. Security. You gotta give it back. Blame me. Tell him it freaks me out.

JAKE: He won't care.

LACEY: Sure it will. He likes me.

JAKE: How do you know that?

LACEY: From the way he looks at me, Jake. He looks at me like he really likes me, okay?

JAKE: Yeah, but that's … that. This is business. Anyway, if he "likes" you so much, he wouldn't want to slit your throat, would he?

LACEY: Not right away. He'd probably do shit to me first.

JAKE: That's not funny.

LACEY: Oh, I know that. So you want me to take it back to him or –

JAKE: No. I'll do it. But tomorrow, okay?

LACEY: Right now.

JAKE: I can't right now. He's having a party.

LACEY: A party. Are you saying you don't wanna spoil his fun or something?

JAKE: No, it's not that. He's just more reasonable when his crew's not around. He thinks they're always looking for signs of weakness in him. You know, in case he needs to be moved out.

LACEY: Moved out? What's that mean?

JAKE: Killed. It means killed.

LACEY: Really? Well, fuck him. And his crew. And whatever the fuck they do in their stupid druggy world. Get it out of here. I mean it.

JAKE: Yeah. I know. I'm sorry.

He starts off, then stops.

JAKE: You all right?

LACEY: I need to lie down.

He approaches her.

JAKE: Okay, but wait up for me, okay?

LACEY: I'll try, yeah.

JAKE: No, don't go to sleep. (*getting closer*) I mean, it's been a while.

LACEY: I know...

JAKE: (*cupping her breast*) I miss you. Stay awake, okay? (*kissing her*) It'll be good.

181

He kisses her again and grabs her ass.

LACEY: Take the drugs back.

JAKE: Okay. But a little later.

> *They kiss again. It gets intense. He is guiding her gently down onto the couch. He has his hand inside her shirt.*

JAKE: I think we should do this first.

LACEY: Yeah ... okay ...

> *She is undoing his jeans.*

JAKE: Yeah. Should I be gentle?

LACEY: Fuck no ...

> *She pulls him in hard. They keep going ...*

> *Blackout.*

SCENE 6

Morning. LACEY, *a little groggy, emerges from the bedroom.*

LACEY: Jake?

Into the kitchen ...

LACEY: Jake? ... What the ...?

A knock on the door and HARRY *comes in.*

HARRY: Okay, seriously. You have to keep that damn door locked. Do you want me to give you a list of why you have to keep it locked? Do you want me to tell you what happened to people who live here when they didn't keep it locked?

LACEY: Some other time, okay? I'm a little upset right now.

HARRY: Why? What happened? It better not be something that could have been avoided by locking that fucking door.

LACEY: Jake's not here.

HARRY: Where is he?

LACEY: I don't know.

HARRY: Is that bad?

LACEY: Maybe.

HARRY: Maybe how bad?

LACEY: Well, I'm not worried he got lost if that's what you mean.

HARRY: Jesus. This not a good time to just disappear.

LACEY: Is there ever?

HARRY: Well, yeah. If things get truly hopeless. But not before you've at least put up a fight.

JAKE comes in carrying a shopping bag.

183

JAKE: Hi.

LACEY: Where the hell have you been?

JAKE: Went out for milk. And tea, just in case our lawyer wanted to pay us a visit. And here he is.

LACEY: You didn't come home last night.

JAKE: Sure I did. You were asleep.

LACEY: No way I'd go to sleep without hearing you come back.

JAKE: I looked in on you. (*to HARRY*) She was out like a light. And I'd only been gone ten minutes.

LACEY: Ten minutes?

JAKE: Maybe less. He wasn't there. I waited a little but –

HARRY: Who wasn't there?

JAKE: No one.

LACEY: No one he wants to talk about. (*looking at HARRY*) What are you doing here anyway?

HARRY: We've got a witness.

JAKE: Really?

HARRY: Oh yeah. And she's going to get on to Mr. SUV right away and ask for two hundred grand. I suggested one hundred, but she's a keener.

LACEY: Is she a communist?

HARRY: No, she's a sociopath. I knew her in law school. A very smart woman. But her only source of pleasure is in fucking with people to the point of total ruin. She's a truly sick but highly functioning individual. She'll say things to him that will scare the shit out of him, and make him question not only her sanity but his own as well. For starters, she'll say she saw him run the light and cause the accident. Which I'm willing to bet is true. That man giving you that cheque means he wants this thing to go away. And whether he did or didn't cause the accident, she's gonna freak him out so much he'll be convinced he's going to wind up in jail for killing your brother anyway.

LACEY: Is she gonna tell him she's a lawyer?

HARRY: There's no upside to that. She'll suggest a public place for him to hand over the money. They'll meet. She'll disappear into the crowd. That's it. Only downside is that she wants twenty percent of whatever she squeezes out of him.

JAKE: How much are you taking?

HARRY: Nothing. That's not who I am now. I no longer profit from the misfortune of others.

LACEY: You're helping us profit from his. I mean, how come no one wants to think about him maybe being innocent?

HARRY: Again, no upside. He pays. Or he doesn't. If he's guilty and has the money, he pays. If he's innocent and has the money, he might still pay just because it's easier. Like I said, I'm betting he is, and he does. And I'm betting that way so you people get something substantial out of this. (*starting out*) I'll be in touch.

He is gone.

LACEY: That's kind of what the detective said to me.

JAKE: What is?

LACEY: That we should try to get something out of this no matter what really happened. Maybe she was trying to set a trap. You know, get me to lie and then –

JAKE: Or maybe she just wants to help us.

LACEY: Yeah, but … well, what the fuck's going on with these people? Why do they care about us all of a sudden? Did anyone care when we were homeless?

JAKE: We were never homeless.

LACEY: We were sleeping on my cousin Karen's floor.

JAKE: Yeah, but we were indoors. Being homeless means you're –

LACEY: Whatever. The point is –

JAKE: No one cared?

LACEY: Until now, yeah. Must be because of the accident.

JAKE: You mean because it got us a lot of attention?

LACEY: And a lot of pity too, I guess.

JAKE: We hate pity.

LACEY: Yes, we fucking do. But if that's all we can get from some people, we should just take it?

JAKE: Definitely.

LACEY: Definitely?

JAKE: Sort of.

LACEY: (*looking at him*) So you actually expect me to believe you were only gone ten minutes last night?

JAKE: It's the truth.

LACEY: Because Darryl wasn't there?

JAKE: He was there, but so was his crew and he wasn't gonna take all that merchandise back from me in front of them.

LACEY: Well, what about now?

JAKE: I texted him. He hasn't gotten back to me yet.

LACEY: Okay. So where are they then?

JAKE: The drugs?

LACEY: Yes, Jake. The drugs.

JAKE: I put them somewhere safe.

LACEY: Where?

JAKE: Doesn't matter. You didn't want them in the apartment, and they're not.

JAKE gets a text.

LACEY: That Daryl?

JAKE: No, it's Clyde.

LACEY: Who the fuck is Clyde?

JAKE: He works for Daryl. He wants a meet-up. I gotta go.

He rushes out.

LACEY: Wait a minute...

JAKE: Can't.

He is gone. LACEY picks up her cellphone and hits a key.

LACEY: (*on the phone*) Hi, Mum. How you doing today?... Worried about what?... No, it's okay. We'll get the money for it somehow... Mum. He's not gonna rot in the morgue, okay?... No, he's not gonna get dumped somewhere either... Yeah, I promise. Please try not to worry about it. I'll call you later. Bye.

She disconnects and puts her head in her hands.

Blackout.

SCENE 7

MR. DAVID and JAKE are both on the couch, fairly close together. MR. DAVID is manspreading with both legs and arms.

JAKE: Do you want me to sit in the chair?

MR. DAVID: No, this is good.

JAKE: It's just that you seem to need a lot of room.

MR. DAVID: Where's Lacey?

JAKE: She's out for a walk.

MR. DAVID: At night? In this neighbourhood?

JAKE: She was born in this neighbourhood.

MR. DAVID: Yeah, but it's changed a lot, right?

JAKE: Not enough to stop her from going for a walk.

MR. DAVID: Good for her. We have to fight back, right?

JAKE: Against who?

MR. DAVID: Against who. That's funny… So, she's feeling better then. And what about you? All these things about the accident haven't caused you to become a little fuzzy-headed?

JAKE: I don't think so.

MR. DAVID: What I'm saying is, I thought we had an agreement. All those zeros on that cheque I gave you…

JAKE: Yeah. That was –

MR. DAVID: Generous. It was very generous.

JAKE: Oh, yeah. For sure.

MR. DAVID: Yes. So this afternoon when I got a call from a woman – whom I assume was representing your interests – asking me for a quarter of a million dollars, I was a little confused.

JAKE: A quarter million. Wow.

MR. DAVID: Yes. A big fucking wow.

JAKE: Only ... what makes you think she was representing us?

MR. DAVID: You mean, why do I have trouble believing that a witness to the accident suddenly appeared and decided on her own to shake me down? Because I'm not a fucking idiot. Do you think I'm a fucking idiot?

JAKE: No.

MR. DAVID: Does your wife?

JAKE: Probably. But that's only because she thinks most men are.

MR. DAVID: What do you know about me?

JAKE: Nothing really.

MR. DAVID: You mean nothing except I drive a very expensive vehicle and can easily spare the sixty thousand dollars I offered you out of the goodness of my heart?

JAKE: It wasn't sixty. It was fifty.

MR. DAVID: Sixty. Fifty. So fucking what? You should have just cashed the cheque! Listen, do you want me to give you a little advice?

JAKE: No. Not really.

MR. DAVID: Well, here it is anyway. Next time you're thinking about shaking someone down, find out much more about that person first. You understand what I'm saying?

JAKE: I think so.

MR. DAVID: You just "think" so?

He casually pulls out a knife.

JAKE: Hey, man. That's not –

> MR. DAVID *stabs himself in his palm, then licks off the blood.*

JAKE: Why'd you do that? What's that mean? Never mind. I don't need to know. Just put it away, okay? I get it. We made a mistake. We'll back off. Please. Weapons aren't the answer, man. If there's a problem that's out of control, let's just work it out. Okay?

MR. DAVID: Sure. I'm good with that. I just wanted you to know where I'm coming from. Do you know where that is now? The place I come from?

JAKE: It's the dark place. You're coming from the dark place I've been trying to stay out of my whole life.

MR. DAVID: No. You know what? I'm pretty sure I'm from a much darker place than that. I'm from a place that's full of death and destruction. A place where there is absolutely no forgiveness, that punishes failure in ways you couldn't even imagine. And if I fail to get you to back off and I'm thrown into the light of day, my punishment will be severe. But before that, before I receive my punishment, I will make sure that both you and your wife are punished in an even worse way. In a way that I'm having trouble picturing without getting sick to my stomach. Is any of this penetrating your very feeble brain?

JAKE: Yeah.

MR. DAVID: Are you sure?

JAKE: Yeah…

MR. DAVID: So… are we all right now? We're cool, yes?

JAKE: Definitely.

MR. DAVID: (*putting the knife away*) So… how long have you and your wife been together anyway?

JAKE: Since we were fifteen.

MR. DAVID: Really? So where are all the children you should have by now?

JAKE: We don't have them.

MR. DAVID: (*smiling*) That's my point. Why not?

JAKE: We're waiting until we're in a better situation.

MR. DAVID: You mean when you're off welfare?

JAKE: We're not on welfare. Getting on welfare would be going backwards.

MR. DAVID: But blackmail is going forward? Do you see the problem with that thinking? How one can make you a loser and the other one a dead loser?

JAKE: Yeah. I do.

MR. DAVID: Good. So this was just a learning situation for you then.

JAKE: Yeah. A learning situation.

MR. DAVID: I understand that. Now cash the cheque, and buy yourself a nice car. It might fool people into thinking you're not just a pathetic nothing. And trust me. That's all you're getting from me. Also, if I get another call like the one I had today ... well I'm going to have to put an end to all this, aren't I? (*standing*) Now do you think you can relay all that was said here to your wife accurately?

JAKE nods.

MR. DAVID: And buy some new furniture, for God's sake. You can't live a good life with junk like this around you. All this evidence of your failures ... It's too much to overcome.

JAKE: (*looking at him*) Did you ... cause the accident?

MR. DAVID: Jake? (*shaking his head*) After all I have just told you, you still want to ask me that question?

JAKE: No, don't worry. I won't tell anyone. No one would believe me anyway. You know, because I'm such a loser.

MR. DAVID: Right.

JAKE: So ... did you?

MR. DAVID just smiles, and leaves.

Blackout.

SCENE 8

LACEY and HARRY. LACEY is dressed in an old track suit of Jake's. JAKE is in the kitchen.

LACEY: She's asking for way too much. You gotta tell her to back off.

HARRY: That's not going to work. She thinks he's a challenge.

JAKE is coming from the kitchen with three mugs.

JAKE: He's a criminal. A serious criminal.

HARRY: Thanks... (*taking a mug*) Yeah. She found that out. And it got her excited. His name's actually Davisomitski, or something like that. He's second-generation Albanian mob. A nasty group of law breakers and she's thrilled about taking them on. Usually she only gets to stick it to sleazy business types and the odd politician. This takes her to a whole new level.

LACEY: Well, it's great that she's having fun, but this guy's threatened us.

JAKE: Me. He threatened me.

LACEY: You, us... What's it matter?

JAKE: Come on. I'd never let him get away with threatening you.

LACEY: (*to HARRY*) He had a gun, so that's probably not true.

JAKE: Actually, it was a knife.

LACEY: You told me it was a gun.

JAKE: In my mind it was a gun.

LACEY: Whatever. I'm not saying you wouldn't have wanted to defend me... (*to HARRY*) He's got a thing about guns.

JAKE: And knives.

HARRY: Irene says that gun and knife stuff is just part of his schtick.

LACEY: Well, tell "Irene" we think killing people might also be part of his schtick. We're happy with the fifty thousand.

HARRY: Doesn't matter. I'm sure he's already put a stop payment on that cheque.

JAKE: Why would he do that?

HARRY: To save money. It was enough to just scare you.

JAKE: Who's scared? I'm not scared.

HARRY: You should be.

LACEY: He is. (*to JAKE*) Look, just take the cheque to the bank, okay? Try to cash it. Then we'll know for sure if we want to do anything else.

HARRY: Yeah, you can't come away from this with nothing.

JAKE: You mean except our lives.

LACEY: Just go to the bank.

JAKE: Sure. But I have a few errands to run so –

LACEY: Do this first. It's in the kitchen drawer with the knives and forks.

> *JAKE retrieves the cheque.*

LACEY: It's made out to me. I'll have to sign the back.

JAKE: (*handing her the cheque*) Right.

HARRY: (*handing LACEY a pen*) This is probably a fool's errand.

LACEY: That's okay. He's a fool.

JAKE: Hey.

LACEY: I'm talking about those other "errands" you have to run.

JAKE: Yeah? Well, that's okay then, I guess.

He takes the cheque and leaves.

HARRY: What's he up to?

LACEY: Shouldn't you be calling Irene?

HARRY: (*taking out his cell and punching a key*) I'll try but...
(*on the phone*) Hi. It's me. Look, you need to step away from
this... Because this man is making my friends very nervous.
(*to* LACEY) She doesn't care.

LACEY grabs his phone.

LACEY: (*on the phone*) Hey. Irene. Back the fuck off. You're
messing with our lives here!... No, it's not worth the risk!...
No, it fucking isn't!

She hands back HARRY's phone.

LACEY: What is it with her?

HARRY: (*shrugging*) Like I told you. She's a sociopath. (*on
the phone*) Irene, look... how about I point you to another
target? We're in a fight with our landlords and we need
someone to go at them in a really big way. This would be a
no-holds-barred situation. Yeah. Total war... (*to* LACEY) She's
considering it.

LACEY: That's big of her.

Blackout.

SCENE 9

LACEY has let ANNIE in. They are both heading to the living room.

ANNIE: You been jogging?

LACEY: Sleeping.

ANNIE: Oh. Well, at least you're getting dressed now.

LACEY: Right. Listen, I've still got nothing to tell you. No new memories. No new need to let myself off the hook. So, whatever you're here for…

ANNIE: There was an incident involving your husband. It was a gang thing in the park near here. And shots were fired –

LACEY: Jesus. Is he dead?

ANNIE: No, he was wounded, but he's going to be okay. He's in the hospital.

LACEY: The hospital. Okay. Yeah… Can you take me there?

ANNIE: Sure, but…

LACEY: (*heading to bedroom*) I'll just get changed…

ANNIE: The thing is, he was with a known dealer who was in possession of a large quantity of crack cocaine. And there were other individuals…

LACEY: (*from off*) What about Jake?

ANNIE: He was shot in the arm.

LACEY comes out of the bedroom unchanged.

LACEY: I meant was he carrying?

ANNIE: No, but – I thought you were going to change.

LACEY: I decided not to bother.

She starts out. ANNIE *follows.*

ANNIE: Look, this was a turf-war kind of thing, so if Jake is involved with these people ...

LACEY: Right. That'd be bad. Got it.

She leaves.

ANNIE: (*following*) Aren't you going to lock the door?

LACEY: (*off*) Jesus Christ. No ...

ANNIE: Not smart. These are not smart people.

ANNIE *leaves and closes the door behind her.*

Blackout.

SCENE 10

MR. DAVID is on the couch, legs spread out and waiting. HARRY comes in.

HARRY: Okay, how many times do I have to ask you to keep that door (*seeing MR. DAVID*) ... locked ...?

MR. DAVID: Hi, there.

HARRY: Who are you?

MR. DAVID: Why do you ask?

HARRY: Well, you're in an apartment that isn't yours.

MR. DAVID: So are you.

HARRY: I'm the ... concierge.

MR. DAVID: The concierge. Is that a joke?

HARRY: Yes.

MR. DAVID: Okay. Good. I liked it.

HARRY: Thanks. Now, who are you?

MR. DAVID: Who do you think I am?

HARRY: I think you're someone who shouldn't be here.

MR. DAVID: Relax. I'm just waiting for that young couple to come home.

HARRY: You can wait in the lobby.

MR. DAVID: Lobby. That must be another joke. There's no couch. Not even a couple of chairs.

HARRY: It's a lobby without furniture.

MR. DAVID: Sure. Because it would all get stolen, wouldn't it? I get that. Come on. Take a load off. Let's chat. I was going to say this to the young people who live here but since you're the ... concierge. Harry, right?

HARRY: Yeah.

MR. DAVID: Right. So actually, you should be the one to receive this information anyway. Irene said it was your idea to approach me.

HARRY: Who's Irene?

MR. DAVID: Please. Don't do that. It will just waste time for both of us.

HARRY: You found her?

MR. DAVID: I never lost her. I had her followed from our meeting.

HARRY: Have you hurt her?

MR. DAVID: Yes.

HARRY: How badly?

MR. DAVID: It's hard to tell. She doesn't seem all that bothered by pain.

HARRY: She isn't. So you might as well let her go.

MR. DAVID: That's one option. What are you anyway? Besides a janitor ... You seem to think of yourself as some kind of hero to the people here. You were a crooked lawyer, right? Is this your attempt at redemption?

HARRY: Could be. Or maybe it's just something that needs to be done.

MR. DAVID: Well, whatever it is, it has to stop. I can't be involved, beyond what I already am, in any of the consequences from that tragic accident. It's already brought me too much attention. I have people to answer to, and they don't like their associates to attract attention. I've already explained this to Jake but apparently you people aren't communicating with each other clearly. So here it is, one last and final fucking time. If I ever hear from any of you again, this "thing" will get truly, truly, truly ugly for all of you. Do you understand what I'm saying?

HARRY: I truly do.

MR. DAVID: Excellent. (*standing*) And tell the young couple that the next bullet Jake takes won't be intended to wound.

HARRY: The next bullet? What are you –

MR. DAVID: You know, if you seriously want to make the people in this place feel better about themselves, put a nice sofa, a few cozy chairs, maybe even a brightly coloured rug in that lobby. Show them you trust that they won't get stolen. Plant new grass around the building. Maybe a few flowering bushes. Small things like that. That's all you should be doing. Anything more ... adventurous is just going to end in heartbreak.

He leaves.

Blackout.

SCENE 11

LACEY, JAKE, and HARRY. JAKE's arm is in a sling. HARRY is on his feet and agitated.

HARRY: He's killed her. I'm sure of it.

JAKE: Should we call the cops?

HARRY: And ask them to look for her body at the bottom of the lake? This man is a seriously deranged criminal. I don't know how high up he's connected but –

LACEY: What's this thing he said about Jake maybe getting shot again?

JAKE: How'd he know about that?

HARRY: My guess is that he supplies Daryl's gang. And he used them to send you a message.

JAKE: Yeah, I was wondering why they all of a sudden turned on me. I don't get it. I'd already told that asshole we wouldn't push it anymore.

LACEY: Then Irene got to work.

HARRY: That was a strategic error.

LACEY: Ours, hers, or his?

HARRY: Mine. I should never have unleashed her. Bless her, she couldn't control her basic instincts. Well, live and learn.

JAKE: If we can.

LACEY: Yeah, we'll have to make sure he knows we're really, really backing off this time. (*to HARRY*) I mean, there's no other choice, is there?

HARRY: Well, there's always another choice. Problem is, we won't know if it was the right one until we make it.

Just letting him threaten us into doing nothing doesn't feel right to me, though. He put a stop payment on that cheque, didn't he?

JAKE: Yeah.

HARRY: Well, there you go. You're getting nothing from that evil asshole if we leave it as is. That settles it.

He starts off.

LACEY: Harry.

HARRY: Don't worry. I'll leave you out of it. And if whatever I do doesn't work out... I've liked getting to know you both very much. You've helped me get focused.

He starts and stops again.

HARRY: One more thing. It's about the petition. Get it signed by as many people as possible. If you have to, just forge their names. No one will notice. Then start the campaign to resist eviction. And please don't give up. Not about that or anything else. How you start off doesn't have to be how you end up.

He leaves.

JAKE: I should go with him.

LACEY: Why?

JAKE: It feels shitty not to. That prick he's going after had me shot.

LACEY: (*sitting on the couch*) So you want a little payback?

JAKE: Maybe.

LACEY: Look, just sit down. You're not that guy.

JAKE: What guy?

LACEY: The one who needs to go get payback and leaves me here worrying about him. Sit down. Please. (*off his look*) Come on. Be that guy, okay? Be my guy.

JAKE looks at her. She pats the couch next to her. He sits. She snuggles up to him.

Blackout.

SCENE 12

LACEY and ANNIE. LACEY is on her feet.

ANNIE: Mr. "David" denies ever seeing your friend.

LACEY: He's lying.

ANNIE: How would Harry even know where to find him?

LACEY: Maybe from Daryl down the hall.

ANNIE: The dealer? The one your husband's involved with?

LACEY: He's not really in – Mr. David is his supplier. Look, I'm not going to talk to you if I think you're just trying to connect Jake to Daryl or any other drug dealer.

ANNIE: You didn't like my heads-up about the company he's keeping? Look, maybe Harry just took a little vacation.

LACEY: A vacation? No way. The man is on a mission.

ANNIE: What?

LACEY: He's trying to get some justice.

ANNIE: For you?

LACEY: For everyone.

ANNIE: Okay. So he's a little unbalanced, then.

LACEY: Maybe. Does that mean we should just forget about him. Look, it's been almost two days. Something's happened to him.

ANNIE: That could be true. But if it's because of who you think it is … Well those guys are good at what they do. And one of the things they do is make people disappear for good.

JAKE comes out of the bedroom in his underwear. He puts his sling back on.

JAKE: What's she doing here?

LACEY: I called her. I'm worried about Harry.

JAKE: He's dead.

LACEY: Maybe.

JAKE: No. For sure. (*to LACEY*) Let me know when she's gone.

He goes back into the bedroom.

ANNIE: What's with him?

LACEY: He's pissed that you told me what went down in the park.

ANNIE: What, he thinks I was gossiping? Jesus... Anyway, let's assume Harry's dead. What's the lesson here, Lacey?

LACEY: The lesson? What the –

ANNIE: The lesson is this: There are individuals out there who shouldn't be messed with. Especially by people with limited resources like you. And –

LACEY: He ran the light. (*off her look*) It came to me last night in bed. I remembered the whole thing. I was driving. I entered the intersection on a green light. I saw him coming out of the corner of my eye, but I thought he'd stop. He didn't. He didn't even slow down. Then it happened. It was freaky and loud. I passed out for a while and then woke up, got out, went to the passenger side, pulled Tim out, and dragged him into the field. And then...

ANNIE: You passed out again.

LACEY: Yeah... But he ran the light. So I want him in jail for killing my brother. But first I wanna take him for a fucking bundle. So we'll both do our thing, okay? You make a case against him. And I'll try to empty his bank account. Tell him. Go tell him you're coming after him.

ANNIE: That's not usually how we go about it.

LACEY: I want him to know as soon as possible that he's not getting away with it.

ANNIE: You mean the accident?

LACEY: Or for doing what he's done to my friend. He was trying to help us! Do you have any fucking idea what that means to me?! Get to work, and put the asshole away.

ANNIE: I'll do my best. And the money you want from him, you'll get that how?

LACEY: I'll think of something.

ANNIE looks worried as she leaves.

Blackout.

SCENE 13

LACEY is asleep on the couch. MR. DAVID *is in the armchair, watching her. She stirs, looks at him, focuses, and sits up.*

LACEY: I knew you'd come.

MR. DAVID: Really? Is that why the door's unlocked?

LACEY: It's always unlocked. Pretty stupid, eh?

MR. DAVID: Where's your husband?

LACEY: At work. I thought we should talk without him. This whole thing is making him very upset.

MR. DAVID: And you think we can make it better with a little talking?

LACEY: You don't wanna talk? You just want to torture me, then kill me?

MR. DAVID: Speaking like that makes you seem a little crazy. Didn't your friend give you my message?

LACEY: No, he did. And I understood. I was ready to do all you wanted. But then he disappeared. And that kinda freaked me out. Freaked me out and shocked me so much that I remembered something.

MR. DAVID: And what was that?

LACEY: (*near tears*) It wasn't your fault. My brother was driving, and he'd had way too much to drink. He went through that red light and you had no choice but to slam into us. I'm really sorry for all we've put you through.

MR. DAVID: What the fuck is wrong with you? What are you talking about?

LACEY: (*smiling*) That's what I'll be telling the cops. And I'll do it ... (*sadly and with tears*) like I just showed you ... (*smiling*)

Everything except my brother being the driver. I can't lay any more grief on my mother. And all you have to do is tell me what you did to my friend Harry. You do that and you'll be in the clear.

MR. DAVID: Sounds like I'm already in the clear.

LACEY: Well, with that version of what happened, you are. There's another one. The real one that says you ran the light. It makes you responsible for my brother's death. It probably puts you in prison.

MR. DAVID: And that's what you just remembered?

LACEY: It's what I'll say I remembered if I have to. So where's Harry?

MR. DAVID: I don't know. The last time I saw him was right here. I gave him a message for you. Did you get it?

LACEY: Yeah...

MR. DAVID: And you didn't understand the part about leaving me alone?

LACEY: Where's Harry?

MR. DAVID: I don't fucking know!

LACEY: I don't believe you!

MR. DAVID: I don't give a shit! Anything else?

LACEY: What?

MR. DAVID: What else... do you... want... from me?!

LACEY: Money.

MR. DAVID: You mean more money.

LACEY: Yeah. A lot more. I mean, it will still be reasonable, but I have to think for a while before I come up with a figure.

MR. DAVID: You mean you don't want to be greedy?

LACEY: That's right. I just want what's fair. I'll be in touch.

MR. DAVID: (*getting very close*) You know, Lacey... I've been restraining myself because I feel sorry for you.

LACEY: Sure you do.

MR. DAVID: (*even closer*) There you go again. Don't fucking think you know me, okay? It's fucking annoying. I'm a very complex individual. And I have tried my best not to hurt you pathetic, ridiculous people. But this thing you're doing... it's very dangerous.

She lies back down.

LACEY: Is it?

He stands.

LACEY: For you or for me?

MR. DAVID: For both of us. Okay. More money. But that's it. It stops with that.

LACEY: (*crossing herself*) Promise.

MR. DAVID: Fuck you.

He gives her a final look, just wondering, then leaves.

Blackout.

SCENE 14

LACEY and JAKE are snuggling on the couch.

JAKE: It was good to see you eat your supper. I've been pretty worried about you.

LACEY: I'm sorry. (*looking at him*) I still need to get stronger though. That detective's right. People who don't have resources are no match for all the assholes out there. So we're gonna take another approach from now on. Not to everything. Just to how we take care of ourselves.

JAKE: It was good of Daryl to take the drugs back.

LACEY: Yeah, he's a saint.

JAKE: I owe him, though.

LACEY: No, you don't.

JAKE: Yeah, Lace, I do. That's just the way things are.

LACEY: Is the door locked?

JAKE: No.

LACEY: Good. Are you nervous?

JAKE: Are you?

LACEY: I'm too mad to be nervous. (*hearing something in the hall*) Shh…

> *They listen, prepare, then: The door swings open. A MASKED MAN storms in, carrying a gun, all in black, including a balaclava. He approaches them, stops, then relaxes his neck muscles.*
>
> *LACEY moves her hand from behind JAKE. She is holding a gun.*

MASKED MAN: No!! No! Don't!!

He whips off the balaclava. It is HARRY.

LACEY: Jesus!

JAKE: What the ...!?

HARRY: Whaddya doing with a gun?!

JAKE: What are you doing –

LACEY: In a mask?!

HARRY: I was just trying to show what could happen if you keep leaving that fucking door unlocked!

LACEY: Where the hell you been, Harry?

HARRY: I needed to keep a low profile while I made some arrangements. (*off gun*) Where did you get that thing?

JAKE: Marco keeps it in the garage. I didn't like the idea but –

LACEY: I thought we should be prepared.

JAKE: It's our new approach to ... certain things.

HARRY: So, you were expecting him to show up?

LACEY: We still are.

HARRY: That's not going to happen.

LACEY: We think it could.

JAKE: She scared him.

HARRY: I killed him. (*off their looks*) Well, did you think I was all talk? That was the old me. This me is much more inclined to add some action to my words.

JAKE: (*to* LACEY) He killed him?

LACEY: That's what he just –

HARRY: How did you scare him?

LACEY: I told him I remembered that he caused the accident.

HARRY: Did he? I mean, did you actually remember that?

LACEY: No.

JAKE: (*to HARRY*) How?

HARRY: How what?

LACEY: How did you kill him?

HARRY: I didn't actually do it myself. I just arranged it. It'll look like a gang killing.

LACEY: You're sure of that?

HARRY: Yes.

JAKE: Why?

HARRY: Because it was. He was squeezing our friend Daryl down the hall for a bigger share. Daryl didn't like that one little bit.

JAKE: And so he did this thing because of that?

HARRY: Plus my promise to keep him in good standing on the premises. He likes it here. And I can help keep the law off his back. (*sitting*) Now, let's talk about the future. How do we get all the people in this building to sign our petition? How do we get them to understand the power they have? How do we get them to understand how important it is to stand up for themselves and push back when their basic life circumstances are threatened? Okay, I can see how you might need some time to consider all that.

He leaves. LACEY *hands* JAKE *the gun.*

JAKE: Can I take that thing back to the garage?

LACEY: You don't think we'll need it again?

JAKE: You heard him. The guy's dead.

LACEY: Yeah, but there are lots of other guys like that out there. I think we should hold on to it for a while.

JAKE: Okay. I guess we should start locking the door too.

LACEY: No way.

JAKE: So, the door will be unlocked. But we'll have a gun. What's that mean?

LACEY: It means ... we're hoping for the best. But we're prepared to blow someone away if we have to. (*kissing him*) That makes sense, doesn't it? I mean, considering how things are ...

JAKE: Out there, you mean?

LACEY: Yeah, out there. And down the hall.

JAKE: Yeah ... (*kissing her neck*) Do you think you're ever gonna remember what happened with the accident?

LACEY: I'm thinking I don't want to. But maybe I should say I do. You know, to do what Harry and the cop said. Blame the asshole.

JAKE: He's dead.

LACEY: Well, he had insurance. And he had money to leave to someone. Why not us?

JAKE: Yeah. Because who knows how long it'll be before you can get back to work?

LACEY: And Marco's never gonna give you a raise.

JAKE: Right. What a prick, eh?

LACEY: And I don't see how my mum ever recovers from Tim dying.

JAKE: Which means we gotta take care of her, put her somewhere nice. And we'll need money for that.

LACEY: A lot. So ... I think I'm starting to remember what happened.

JAKE: That's good.

LACEY: But I've heard insurance companies fight like hell not to pay anyone anything. And if he had a family they're probably evil assholes like he was. So just me saying it was his fault won't be enough. We need to find a witness.

JAKE: You mean a real witness?

LACEY: Or just, you know... a witness.

They think, look at each other, then smile.

Blackout.

THE END

GEORGE F. WALKER is one of Canada's most prolific and popular playwrights. He has written more than thirty plays and created screenplays for several award-winning Canadian TV series. Part Franz Kafka, part Lewis Carroll, Walker's distinctive, gritty, fast-paced comedies satirize the selfishness, greed, and aggression of contemporary urban culture. Among his best-known works are *Gossip* (1977); *Zastrozzi, the Master of Discipline* (1977); *Criminals in Love* (1984); *Better Living* (1986); *Nothing Sacred* (1988); *Love and Anger* (1989); *Escape from Happiness* (1991); *Suburban Motel* (1997, a series of six plays set in the same motel room); and *Heaven* (2000). Since the early 1980s, he has directed most of the premieres of his own plays.

During a ten-year absence from theatre, he mainly wrote for television, including the TV series *Due South*, *The Newsroom*, *This Is Wonderland*, and *The Line*, as well as for the film *Niagara Motel* (based on three plays from his *Suburban Motel* series). Walker returned to the theatre with *And So It Goes* (2010). Since that time, he has published *King of Thieves* (2013), *Dead Metaphor* (2015, a series of three plays that includes *Dead Metaphor*, *The Ravine*, and *The Burden of Self Awareness*), and *Moss Park and Tough! The Bobby and Tina Plays* (2015). *We the Family* (2016) looks at the after-effects of a wedding between culturally divergent families, whereas *After Class* (2017) gathers two plays, *Parents Nights* and *The Bigger Issue*, about the failing education system.

Walker's awards and honours include investiture as a Member of the Order of Canada (2005); the National Theatre School of Canada's Gascon-Thomas Award (2002); two Governor General's Literary Awards for Drama; five Dora Mavor Moore Awards; nine Floyd S. Chalmers Canadian Play Awards; and the Governor General's Lifetime Artistic Achievement Award.